MODEM
CONNECTIONS
BIBLE

Carolyn Curtis
Daniel L. Majhor

MODEM CONNECTIONS BIBLE

Howard W. Sams & Co., Inc.
A Subsidiary of Macmillan, Inc.
4300 West 62nd Street, Indianapolis, Indiana 46268 U.S.A.

International Standard Book Number: 0-672-22446-1
Library of Congress Catalog Card Number: 85-72106

Edited by: *Katherine Stuart Ewing*
Illustrations by: *Tom Emrick*

Printed in the United States of America

Contents

Appendixes

Acknowledgments

We would like to thank Kim Maxwell, founder of Racal-Vadic, and also John Bingham, who invented the 1200-bit-per-second modem in 1972, for making this kind of book possible. A special thanks to the people who have helped us in so many ways during our data communications careers and specifically with the cooperation and information necessary to prepare this book. Thanks especially to Tony Gerbic, Karl Zorzi, Steve Clary, Keith Peters, Randy Louie, Carlos Laux, and Bart Anderson. Also a bouquet to the fine folks at Mission Peak Systems in Hayward, who were very helpful with information about the Osborne 1. To the crew at The Waite Group, thanks to Mike Van Horn for finding us, to Mary Johnson for her editing and encouragement, and to Kim House for his critiques of our drawings and the information for Appendix E.

All terms mentioned in this book that are known to be trademarks or service marks are listed below. In addition, terms suspected of being trademarks or service marks have been appropriately capitalized. Howard W. Sams & Co., Inc., cannot attest to the accuracy of this information. Use of a term in this book should not be regarded as affecting the validity of any trademark or service mark.

Access II, Apple IIc, IIe, II+, Applesoft, and Appleterm are registered trademarks, and Macintosh, MacTerminal, and MacGeorge are trademarks of Apple Computer, Inc.

ASCII Express is a trademark of United Software Industries, Inc.

AT&T, AT&T Bell 103, and Bell are registered trademarks of AT&T Information Systems.

BRS/Search is a registered trademark and BRS/After Dark is a trademark of BRS Information Technologies.

Commodore 64 is a trademark of Commodore Business Machines, Inc.

COMPAQ is a trademark of COMPAQ Computer Corp.

CompuServe is a registered trademark of CompuServe Corp.

CP/M is a registered trademark of Digital Research Corporation.

Crosstalk is a trademark of Microstuf Inc.

Dow Jones News/Retrieval is a registered trademark of Dow Jones & Co., Inc.

Eagle is a registered trademark of Eagle Computers, Inc.

Easynet is a service mark of Telebase Systems Inc.

Epson is a trademark of Epson America, Inc.

Freeware is a trademark of Headlands Communications Corporation.

GEORGE is a trademark of RD Communications, Inc.

GRid Compass is a trademark of GRid Systems Corporation.

GTE and Telenet are trademarks of GTE Telenet Communications Corp.

Hayes, Micromodem, Smartcom, and Smartmodem are registered trademarks of Hayes Microcomputer Products, Inc.

IBM, IBM PC AT, IBM PC, PCjr, and IBM PC XT are registered trademarks of International Business Machines Corporation.

In-Search is a trademark of Menlo Corp.

Kaypro is a trademark of Kaypro Corporation.

Kermit is copyrighted by Columbia University.

Lattice is a registered trademark of Lattice, Inc.

Lotus is a trademark of Lotus Development Corporation.

MCI Mail is a trademark of MCI Corp.

Mead, Nexis, and Lexis are trademarks of Mead Data Central.

Microsoft and MS-DOS are registered trademarks of Microsoft, Inc.

Morrow is a registered trademark of Morrow Designs, Inc.

MITE is a trademark of Mycroft Labs Inc.

NewsNet is a trademark of Independent Publications, Inc.

Novation Smart-Cat is a trademark of Novation Inc.

Osborne is a registered trademark of Osborne Computer Corporation.

Panasonic is a registered trademark of Panasonic.

PC-DOS is a trademark of International Business Machines Corporation.

PC-Talk is a trademark of Headlands Communications Corp.

pfs Access is a trademark of Software Publishing Corp.

Popcom is a trademark of Prentice Corporation.

Racal-Vadic is a trademark of RD Communications Inc.

Radio Shack and Tandy are registered trademarks of Radio Shack/Tandy Corporation.

Relay is a trademark of VM Personal Computers.

Seequa Chameleon is a trademark of Seequa Computer Corp.

Sprint is a registered trademark of GTE Sprint Corporation.

Tymnet is a trademark of Tymshare Inc.

U.S.Robotics Password is a trademark of U.S.Robotics Inc.

Visicorp is a trademark of Visicorp, Inc.

Volksmodem is a trademark of Anchor Automation, Inc.

WordStar is a registered trademark of MicroPro International Corp.

1

How To Use This Book

The Purpose of This Book

The purpose of *Modem Connections Bible* is to enable people to connect a modem to a microcomputer without worrying. Unlike other peripherals, such as printers, modems are generally purchased some time after the computer is bought. They may well be purchased from a different store or from mail order. This situation can present problems when you need advice or even a cable to connect the two pieces of equipment.

Most modems for microcomputers are stand-alone units, separate from the computer. These modems have connectors known as RS-232-C interfaces. Thus these modems should work with any computer that also has an RS-232-C interface. However, for two reasons, connecting modems and computers isn't as simple as it sounds.

First, all RS-232-C interfaces aren't the same, which may come as a shock to those people who believe that the phrase "RS-232-C standard" promises that these interfaces have some degree of uniformity. Hardware manufacturers have implemented the standard to suit their particular needs.

The second problem is that between the stand-alone modem and the computer's RS-232-C interface is a cable, which must be exactly the right kind. A friend of the writers worked from his computer's documentation to construct his own cable. The results were smoke, damage to the computer, and a $200 bill at a computer repair shop.

This book is meant to preserve you, your computer, and your modem from a similar fate. The heart of the book is a collection of drawings of the RS-232-C interfaces on a number of popular microcomputers, the interfaces on the modems, and the cables that connect the two. The pins and sockets on the interfaces and the various wires of the cables are labeled with the initials of the various RS-232-C functions.

Who Should Read This Book

The *Modem Connections Bible* was written for three groups:

1. People who have one or more microcomputers and one or more modems and want to get the computers and the modems to work together

2. People who are thinking of buying a modem and want to know what kind they should get

3. People who want to know something about how modems work

If you are in the first group, you'll use Chapter 5 and the Jump Table extensively. Appendixes B, *The RS-232-C Interface*, and E, *Troubleshooting* are also available if you need more help.

If you are in the second group, you'll learn in Chapter 2 about the kinds of modems available and in Chapter 4 about software. Appendix A describes ways to use modems, ways of which you might not have thought. The reading list, Appendix C, provides additional food for thought. The many specific applications outlined in Chapters 2 and 4 can help you narrow down your requirements and make the right purchase.

Chapters 2 and 3 are for the third group. Appendix D is a reference tool. The reading list in Appendix C lists places to look for more information.

What This Book Covers

Modems—like religion and cooking—are too interesting a topic to be relegated to experts. This book may not make an expert out of you but will explain, in a nontechnical way:

what the initials of the RS-232-C functions stand for

how a modem talks with the computer to which the modem is attached

how a modem establishes contact with another modem

how data has to be changed so that it can go over the telephone line

how modems can send data at speeds much faster than the 300 baud, or bits per second (bps), that used to be the standard speed

what the word *baud* really means

what a COM port is

what a UART is

how error checking works

These matters are covered in the main chapters of the book. The Jump Table in Chapter 5 is a quick way to access the charts and drawings in that chapter. Many computers and modems work alike. If this book has no drawing of the combination you want, the Jump Table can direct you to a combination that works. The appendixes also help you find answers quickly.

The Arrangement of This Book

Following this introductory chapter, you'll find four more chapters and six appendixes, the contents of which are summarized in the next few paragraphs.

Chapter 2, *Hardware Basics*, starts with explanations of the essential communications equipment: modems, cables, adapter boards, connectors, and ports. This chapter details the kinds of modems on the market, with an eye toward helping you to choose a modem that suits your needs. It explains the way modems work, based on the type.

Chapter 3, *A Call's Progress*, is devoted to the RS-232-C interface as used by modems and microcomputers. The third chapter shows you in detail the sequence of events that starts when you ask your modem to place a call. At this point you find out what the initials on the pins in Chapter 5's charts stand for.

Chapter 4, *Communications Software*, tells you what communications software does and why you need it. The chapter describes many features available today in communications programs, starting with the essentials and proceeding to the latest wrinkles, which almost achieve the sophistication of electronic mail. This chapter ends on a practical note, describing several typical uses of modems and software and detailing what features to look for.

Chapter 5, *Charts and Drawings,* is the core of this book. Each drawing shows a major microcomputer or personal computer and a major stand-alone modem, the interfaces on each, and the cable that should connect the computer and the modem. The chart shows the functions of the pins on the interface and how they are connected through the cable. The Appendixes contain reference material as follows:

Appendix A, *Call Me, Modem,* describes what you can call with your modem: online services or information utilities; electronic databases; and a new development, gateway services, that makes both of the preceding easier to use. Included is a brief exploration of the fees for entering this wonderland.

Appendix B, *The RS-232-C Interface,* is a table of the various functions of the 25 pins on the RS-232-C interface. The pins used by modems are printed in boldface for convenient reference.

Appendix C, *Further Reading: A Select List of Books,* presents a few of the many excellent books on online services. Listed also are some books on data communications in general.

Appendix D, *Glossary,* defines communications hardware and software terms used in this book.

Appendix E, *Troubleshooting,* provides help when things seem to be going wrong. Some tools you may use to monitor interfaces and to construct your own cables are described also.

Appendix F, *Communications Software for Microcomputers,* provides a list of commonly available programs for use with particular microcomputers.

2

Hardware Basics

A *modem* enables a computer to use telephone lines to exchange information with another computer. Modems do this by changing the signals that a computer produces into a form that can be sent over telephone lines, then changing the signal from the telephone line back into a form that can be used by the computer at the other end.

Several transformations are involved here. Information in the computer, both commands and data, is parallel and digital. *Parallel* means that the information is coded in bits and passed on 8, 16, or 32 bits at a time. A *byte*, which is made up of eight bits, might look like the following:

00101101

This collection of bits would be passed as one byte in an 8-bit machine. If the computer were a 16-bit or 32-bit machine, the units would be a 16- or 32-bit word. *Digital* relates to the fact that the words are made up of bits which are either on or off, one or zero.

Phone lines, on the other hand, are not designed (at least they didn't used to be) to handle information in chunks like data bytes in digital form. On a phone line, the sounds and signals transmitted vary in frequency and length. This variation can be thought of as *analog*: the information is not being passed as discrete ones or zeros.

The phone lines also pass information in *serial* rather than parallel form. When a byte is sent over the phone line, it goes one bit at a time. Thus, to go over the telephone line, information from a computer must be transformed from its parallel form into serial form and from its digital form into analog form. The modem at the outgoing end makes these transformations, and the modem at the other end reverses them for the receiving computer.

Electronically speaking, the modem changes the computer signals for the telephone line by *modulating* and *demodulating* them—hence, the name *modem*. Different forms of modulation exist, and the forms have a bearing on modem speeds. We go into more detail when we describe modem speeds. We also look at the serial format used in microcomputer communications, which is *asynchronous*.

Types of Modems

Before we look closely at how modems work their magic, let's investigate the different types of modems available on the market, with a view to helping you decide what will best suit your needs. The different ways modems are categorized include the following:

How they connect to computers (stand-alone, internal, and integral modems, or acoustic coupled modems)

The kind of telephone lines they use (switched network modems vs. leased line modems)

Their sophistication (manual dial versus autodial/auto answer, originate-only vs. originate/answer)

The speeds at which modems send information (300, 1200, and 2400 bits per second)

Connections

Stand-Alone Modems

A *stand-alone modem* is housed in a flat, oblong metal or plastic box that is usually an appropriate size to sit underneath a regular telephone. Inside the flat box is a printed circuit board. The front end of the box may have various indicator lights, usually LEDs (light-emitting diodes).

At the rear of the stand-alone modem are sockets for three or four connections.

The connection to an electrical outlet involves a power supply. The electrical requirements for the modem usually are not included on the printed circuit board inside the box because of the heat that the power supply components generate. Some modem power supplies are designed to plug directly into an electrical outlet. Most power supplies, however, are heavy black boxes, a few cubic inches in size, with a power cord coming out either side. One cord has the connector for the modem. The

Fig. 2-1.   Generic stand-alone modem.

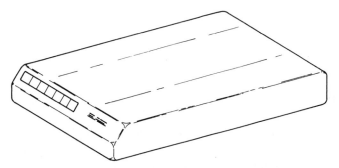

Fig. 2-2.   Stand-alone modem sockets.

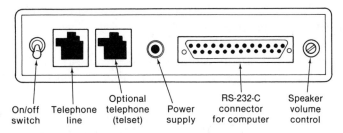

On/off   Telephone   Optional   Power   RS-232-C   Speaker
switch   line   telephone   supply   connector   volume
              (telset)   for computer   control

other cord has a three-pronged plug for the electrical outlet.

You may have seen some stand-alone modems that include two cups into which a standard telephone receiver and transmitter will fit snugly. These modems receive and send actual sound waves through the telephone handset. Stand-alone modems, in contrast to others we describe in following text, are *direct connect* modems and send electrical pulses through the telephone line.

Acoustic Coupled Modems   *Acoustic coupled modems* are used with a telephone line that does not have a modular outlet. Modular outlets, also called phone jacks, accept the little plastic plugs that you see at the ends of standard telephone cables these days. Most modems now use the same type of connectors.

Fig. 2-3.   Acoustic coupler.

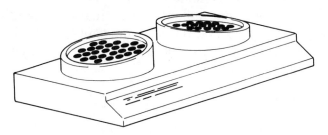

Although fewer and fewer nonmodular telephone outlets are left, particularly in the sort of high-tech locations where modems are likely to be used, the phones in hotel and motel rooms still are apt to be non-modular because that type is less easy to steal. Therefore, travelers using modems may need to use acoustic couplers.

Acoustically coupled modem models available conform to the following standards:

Bell 103, which transmits at 300 bits per second

Vadic 3400, which transmits at 300 or 1200 bits per second

Bell 202, half duplex, 0 to 1200 bits per second, which exchange data only with another Bell 202

Note the absence of the commonly used Bell 212A standard (1200 bits per second) from this group. Speeds are discussed in more detail later in this chapter.

For most businesses and homes, direct connect modems are more advantageous than acoustically coupled modems. Direct contact modems exclude much better any extraneous signals and noise. If you don't have a modular telephone outlet, contact your telephone company about converting to modular so that you can use a direct connect modem.

Local telephone companies may require information such as type, name of manufacturer, equipment model number, FCC registration number, and ringer equivalance number, which can be found in the modem's documentation or on the modem's identification plate.

European Modem Connections In most of Europe, the situation is different from that in the United States. Telephone service is part of the (excellent) postal service. Acoustic modems are the ones sold in computer stores. Direct connect modems usually are available only from the government-owned telephone service.

The same situation existed in the United States until 1969 when the Federal Communications Commission implemented the Carterphone decision, allowing non-Bell modems to be connected to the telephone system. To protect Bell's equipment, the company required modems to include a device called a Data Access Arrangement, but this device was eliminated when the FCC instituted a certification program for all modems, including Bell's, in 1977.

Internal Modems

An *internal modem* is a printed circuit board that is designed to work inside a particular computer. If your computer is one that a lot of other computers are compatible with, such as the IBM PC, chances are good that an internal modem designed for that computer will work also inside its compatibles.

Note that computer compatibility is a relative term. When an internal modem is said to work inside Computer X "and compatibles," what is meant is *operational compatibility*, which means that major software intended for Computer X will run on the compatibles with no problems. Computer X can read disks written to by the compatible and vice versa. Add-on boards, such as internal modems, that are designed for Computer X can be used inside the compatibles.

In contrast to a stand-alone modem, an internal modem usually has only two connectors. These are visible on the portion exposed through the back of the computer in which the internal modem is installed. One jack is for the cable that plugs into the telephone line. The other jack is for a cable to an optional telephone handset.

Internal modems derive power from the computer in which they are housed, so they don't need a power supply. They communicate directly with the computer, so no serial port or RS-232-C interface is needed.

If your computer comes with a serial port and a modem, you can use the port for devices other than the modem. If the computer doesn't come with a serial port, you will have to buy an asynchronous adapter board (async board, for short) for your internal modem. The universal asynchronous receiver-transmitter (UART) that is the heart of an async board is included on an internal modem. (UARTs are described later in this chapter.)

Integral Modems

Integral modems are included in certain computers, especially lap-size portables like the HP 110, Tandy 100 and 200, GRiD Compass, and some models of the Data General One. Except for the integral modem in the GRiD Compass, these modems usually produce only 300 bps, but the day is coming when more integral modems will be capable of higher speeds.

Which Is Best?

First, keep in mind that not all computers can accept internal modems. The Macintosh, Apple IIc, and Sanyo MBC 555 can't. Of course, the lap-size portables can't, although they already may have an integral modem. In addition, some computers have just one slot for an add-on board, and you may wish to put something else in that slot.

If you do have a choice between a stand-alone and an internal modem, you should decide based on adaptability to a computer you may buy later, convenience (portability and space consumption), software, cables, and cost.

Adaptability   If you buy a stand-alone modem for your computer, chances are that you will be able to get the stand-alone to work with another type of computer, assuming that you have the proper cable and software. On the other hand, an internal modem can be used only in the type of computer for which that modem was designed. Sometimes this "type" consists of one model of one computer, but sometimes the type applies to quite a number of machines, such as the IBM PC operationally compatible computers.

Convenience   If you have a portable computer or are going to be moving your computer around a lot, an internal modem makes the most sense: there is no extra box to carry around, no power supply, just a telephone cable to tuck in your pocket. Likewise, if there isn't much room where you have your computer set up or electrical outlets are limited, your modem should be inside your computer. On the other hand, if you have filled or plan to fill all the slots in your computer with other add-on boards, you have to get a stand-alone modem.

Software   An internal modem, designed as it is for a specific computer, is usually packaged with software that will run on that computer. Stand-alone modems generally are not marketed for a specific computer, however, and therefore do not include software. See Chapter 4 to find out what software is available to drive specific stand-alone modems.

Cables   Like software, a cable is not generally included with a stand-alone modem because the manufacturer cannot know with what computer you will use the modem. Chapter 5 shows cables for a number of computer-modem combinations. To find the combination you need, use the Jump Table at the beginning of Chapter 5. You should be able to buy cables from your computer dealer if your computer and modem are popular brands.

Cost   A 1200-bps stand-alone and a 1200-bps internal modem from the same manufacturer usually have about the same cost, although the stand-alone may cost slightly more. In addition, the stand-alone will require a cable and software and may require an async adapter board or serial card for the computer. As of this writing, some prices for these additional parts are as follows:

cable: $20 to $50

software: free to $200

async board: $100

total: $120 to $350

Telephone Lines

Some modems can use regular telephone lines, known as the dialup or switched network, and other modems use leased (private) lines. Modems for leased lines use a different connection protocol from the switched network modems. Because a leased telephone line has much less distortion than a regular phone line, a modem for a leased line can transmit information at much higher speeds. Unfortunately, both the leased telephone line and the high-speed modem are quite expensive at the present time. They are used primarily by large companies with mainframe computers and a need to transmit large amounts of information rapidly and accurately. Because this book focuses on modems that can be used by most people who own or work with personal computers, we concentrate on modems that use the switched network phone lines available to all of us.

Sophistication

Autodial versus Manual

The majority of modems described in this book are *autodial* modems. With these modems, you simply type on the computer's keyboard the telephone number you want. Autodial modems enable sophisticated modem software to store telephone numbers for such purposes as dialing through a list of numbers in a particular order, dialing a number automatically at a time you specify, and redialing a number that is frequently busy.

Manual connect modems must have a telephone connected to the other telephone jack on the modem in order for a telephone number to be dialed. Telephone numbers cannot be stored by these modems. Still, manual connect modems will send data from your computer through the telephone line and receive data sent to the computer, and they are relatively inexpensive. If you are going to use your modem only to dial one particular number, such as another private computer, you may be able to get by with a cost-saving manual modem.

Originate-Only versus Originate/Answer

Originate-only modems only dial out. You cannot set them up to answer incoming calls. Although you may not be able to imagine why you would want to set up your modem to answer calls, it still makes sense to get a modem that can both call and answer because the cost is virtually the same as for an originate-only modem. The major modems discussed in this book all have originate/answer capability.

Modem Speeds

Modem speeds—the rates at which modems transmit data through a telephone line—are expressed in terms of *bits per second* or *bps*. This is sometimes also called *baud rate*, which is somewhat misleading, as we shall see. Here we use the term *bps*.

Each letter or other character sent through the modem usually is encoded into 10 bits. Thus, a modem that transmits at 300 bps can send 30 characters per second to the other system. Likewise, 1200 bps and 2400 bps come out to 120 and 240 characters per second, respectively.

The first modems generally available for personal computers transmitted information at speeds up to 300 bits per second. Now, however, 1200 bps is becoming the speed used most frequently. Modems capable of 2400 bps are on the market as well, and they do not cost much more money than the 1200-bps modems. Those 2400-bps modems can also transmit at 1200 and 300 bps. A fast modem can operate at slower speeds if necessary. You can communicate with online services, such as the Source and Dow Jones News/Retrieval Service, at 300, 1200, and in major population centers at 2400 bps. Most free bulletin boards can be accessed at 300 and 1200 bps also, and more and more will be using 2400 bps too. To be sure, leased-line modems can transmit data at speeds up to 19,200 bps, but switched network modems, traditionally called low-speed modems, are closing the gap. Look for affordable 4800- and 9600-bps modems for personal computers in the near future.

What Speed Should You Get?

The speed at which you will require your modem to transmit depends on your application. Both practical and financial factors must be considered before making your purchase. Practical considerations include the fact that at 300 bps, material will roll across your screen at a sedate pace that you'll be able to read with little effort, which is just fine for reading your messages on CompuServe, the Source, or Dial-a-Match. At 1200 bps, very few speed readers can keep up with the screen display. Still, if you're communicating with a system that pauses after each screenful or are capturing material for later use anyway, 1200 bps may be appropriate. You'll find that if you receive a lot of material, especially if you're storing it for later use, 300 bps can be maddeningly slow. You can save a lot of thumb-twiddling by using 1200 bps or 2400 bps if both systems support the appropriate speed.

If you're going to receive material that always takes a long time to send, like graphics, the faster your modem can get the information to you, the more productive you'll be. Such a use makes you a candidate for the 2400-bps category, if the system sending you the material can transmit at that speed.

If you intend to print out most of what you receive as it comes in, your printer may be the determining factor. How many characters per second can your printer print—30, 120, or 240?

You also should consider financial factors when thinking about buying a modem. At present, modems that operate at 1200 bps are approximately twice as expensive as 300-bps modems, and 2400-bps modems are typically another $200. In addition, some online services charge a higher rate for 1200-bps and 2400-bps transmission. On the other hand, these charges typically are *not* four and eight times the cost of 300-bps transmission, so after a while, your 1200-bps modem may pay for itself in reduced connect time charges. These charges include both those of the telephone company and those that might be levied by the system with which you are communicating. If you are communicating over long stretches of time with a faraway system, you probably should get a 1200- or 2400-bps modem.

How Modems Work

Now that we have looked at the different types of modems, we should discuss how these devices work before we look at the other equipment used in computer communications.

Asynchronous and Serial

Most modems for personal computers transmit material *asynchronously*. That is, the receiving system is not *synchronized* with the sending system. The material is sent character by character, and an indeterminate amount of time can pass between the sending of one character and another. We shall see a way to tell when a character is starting and ending.

Besides being asynchronous, modem communication is *serial*: information must be sent one bit at a time because a telephone line is not set up for parallel transmission. Telephone lines really weren't set up for data transmission at all, but modem companies have found various adroit ways around that fact. Furthermore, the switched telephone network is beginning to be digitized. Phone lines capable of sending data as well as a regular voice conversation simultaneously are being test marketed as we write this book.

Ones, Zeros, and Bits

Computer data is transmitted as *data bits*. These data bits might form a code for a letter of the alphabet, numeral, other printable character (such as &), or nonprinting character (such as a carriage return). The most commonly used code for text is seven-bit ASCII (ASCII stands for American Standard Code for Information Interchange and was set up by the Electronics Institute of America). A code using eight data bits is also frequently used. The additional 128 characters that an eight-data-bit code provides might be graphics or other special characters, or the eighth data bit might convey word-processing codes. Of course, the eight data bits may signify something other than text, such as instructions in a computer program.

How would a character be transmitted? Use capital B as an example. In seven-bit ASCII, capital B is ASCII value 66 decimal, or 42H (hexadecimal). Usually, this number in the binary numbering system would be printed with its most significant bit on the left and its least significant bit on the right. We are printing the number the other way around, for reasons that will become clear in following text.

LSB   MSB
0 1 0 0 0 0 1

The ones and zeros of the binary numbering system are transmitted as voltage, set by the RS-232-C standard as:

sending   receiving
0 = +3 to + 25 V   = +5 to + 15 V
1 = −3 to − 25 V   = −5 to − 15 V

Note that the voltage sent has a much wider range than the voltage received.

Our letter B can be drawn as

Fig. 2-4. **High and low to match zeros and ones.**

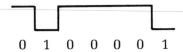

0 1 0 0 0 0 1

Note: Zero is positive and is shown here as "high"!

In async communication, computers "need to know" when a character is coming and where its end is. Thus, in addition to these seven bits that convey the meaning, a character must be preceded by a *start bit* and followed by one or two *stop bits*. The start bit is a logical zero and the stop bit is a logical one. As you might infer from the start bit being a zero, the system *idles* at logic 1 (low voltage),

Fig. 2-5. **High and low to match ones and zeros.**

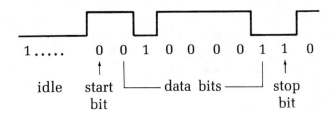

1 . . . . .   0 0 1 0 0 0 0 1 1 0

idle   start ⌐———— data bits ————⌐ stop
         bit   bit

Figure 2-6 summarizes the values of one and zero so far.

A *parity bit* also may be sent. The parity bit provides a simple form of error checking. The most common types of parity are *even* and *odd*. In our example of the letter B, you will notice that two ones are included. In even parity, the parity bit would be a zero to make an even sum of two ones. In

Fig. 2-6.   Summary of one and zero values.

EIA zero (0)	=	HIGH or ON	=	SPACE	=	receive +5 to +15V	=	send +3 to +25V	=	start bit always 0
EIA one (1)	=	LOW or OFF	=	MARK	=	receive −5 to −15V	=	send −5 to −25V	=	stop bit always 1

odd parity, to keep the sum of ones odd (here, three) the parity bit for the letter B would be a one. The parity bit is sent before the stop bit:

Fig. 2-7.   High and low to match ones and zeros.

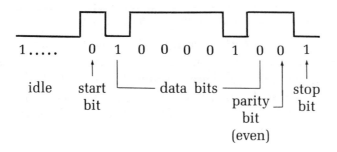

If the character is sent incorrectly, chances are fifty-fifty that the odd or even parity bit will show that something is awry. For instance, if sender and receiver have agreed on even parity, a character that transmits with five ones indicates that an error in transmission has occurred. Of course, another possibility is for the parity bit to be sent incorrectly. Bear in mind also that the parity bit does not correct errors but merely provides a (less than bulletproof) method of error checking.

The other choices for parity besides odd and even are *mark* and *space*, both rarely used, and *no parity*. Mark parity means that the parity bit is always set to one. Space parity means that the parity bit is always set to zero. The only function for these settings is to take up room. The terms *mark* and *space* come from the days of the telegraph.

A setting of *no parity* is common when eight data bits are used because a sum of ten bits per character is usual. If no parity bit is included, but seven data bits are used, two stop bits usually are used to make a sum of ten bits per character. Following are the most typical settings:

One start bit, seven data bits, even parity, one stop bit

One start bit, eight data bits, no parity, one stop bit

The shorthand notation for these settings, which you'll see when online systems are discussed, is 7E1 and 8N1, respectively. The start bit requirement rarely varies, so it doesn't need to be specified.

Figure 2-8 shows how our letter B, sent with the setting 7E1, would look if you were monitoring the serial port.

Fig. 2-8.   Letter B with setting 7E1.

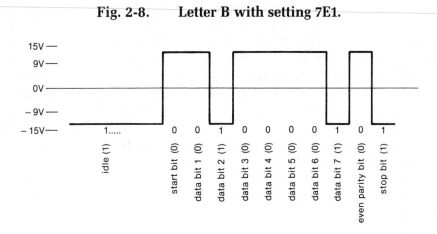

The Difference Between bps and Baud

Many communications software and modem manufacturers, to say nothing of people who write books and articles about communications for personal computers, use the terms *baud* and *baud rate* interchangeably with the term *bps*. Because people who use *baud* correctly are definitely in the minority, you can get along without knowing what baud really means. However, understanding the meaning shows you the ingenious ways that modem designers have surmounted the limitations of sending data through the telephone lines.

Baud rate designates the number of signal changes occurring on a line during a given time period and has to do with the way the modem modulates the signal from the computer. Examples of different baud rates are found among the main types of modems for personal computers.

Commercially available modems using the speeds 300, 1200, and 2400 bps adhere to certain standards: AT&T Bell 103 (0-300 bps), Bell AT&T 212A and Vadic 3400 (1200 bps), and V.22 bis, an international standard set by the Consultative Committee for International Telegraphy and Telephony (2400 bps).

Direction

Before we look at speeds more closely, we need to look at the *direction* a modem is sending data. Is it all going one way, two ways, or both ways at the same time? The terms *full duplex* and *half duplex* come into play here. Personal computer communications are typically full duplex, like the telephone line itself. Full duplex means that if someone telephones you, the caller can talk and listen and so can you. If you want, the two of you can talk simultaneously. If you imagine a phone system wherein only one of you could talk at a time, and you had to tell the other person when to take his or her turn to speak ("over to you"), that would be half duplex.

Actually, half duplex would work fine for personal computer communications if a few minor details were worked out. The reason why they haven't been worked out can be traced back to the first uses of switched-network modems. Bell developed them in the sixties for use with terminals, which always were connected to computers with separate channels for sending and receiving. It made sense to make these terminals' modems full duplex so that the modems worked with existing hardware interfaces and software.

The requirement that a personal computer modem be able to send and receive data at the same time means that the data link—that is, the two computers, their modems, and the telephone line that joins computer to modem—uses two channels: one on which the originating modem sends data, and one on which the answering modem sends data.

Frequencies and Bandwidth

The telephone network will accommodate a range of frequencies from 300 to 3300 Hertz (cycles per second, abbreviated Hz), which creates an effective bandwidth (range of frequencies) of 3000 Hz. Modems with different bps and baud rates use these frequencies in different ways.

300 bps, 300 Baud The standard type of 300-bps modem, AT&T Bell 103, sends ones and zeros by a technique known as *frequency shift keying*. A modem conforming to the Bell 103 standard can send 300 bits per second this way. Because each bit is a signal change, 300 bps is also 300 baud.

An originating modem sends a zero to the receiving modem by transmitting a frequency or waveform of 1070 Hz. Originating modems send a one by transmitting at 1270 Hz. If the modem at the other end tries to send some information at the same time the originating modem is sending, the answering modem sends its zeros at 2025 Hz and its ones at 2225 Hz. In summary:

	originating modem	answering modem
send	1070 zero	2025 zero
	1270 one	2225 one
receive	2025 zero	1070 zero
	2225 one	1270 one

According to transmission theory, frequency shift keying requires a bandwidth of 1.5 Hz per signal change (baud). A pair of 103 standard modems sends 300 baud each way, for a total of 600 baud. That total of 600 multiplied by 1.5 gives 900 Hz, which is well within the 3000 Hz bandwidth provided by the telephone company.

1200 bps, 600 Baud If a modem sent 1200 signal changes, the product of (1200 baud + 1200 baud) × 1.5 would be 3600 Hz, which would not fit the telephone network's bandwidth. Therefore, 1200-bps modems use a form of *phase shift keying* rather than frequency shift keying. The carrier frequencies for originate and answer remain within the telephone bandwidth, but these signals, which may be thought of as waves, are manipulated (modulated) in another way.

In addition to frequency (how many waves per second) and amplitude (how high/low the peaks and valleys of the waves are), waves have another quality: *phase*. Look at a regular succession of waves (see Fig. 2-9).

Fig. 2-9.   Regular succession of waves.

Looking at Figure 2-9, you could note whether a delay or speedup occurs if you had some way of marking the point when the top of the wave is supposed to appear (see Fig. 2-10).

Fig. 2-10.   Waves with delay.

A 1200-bps modem puts an electronic marker on the signal that the modem is receiving from the other modem, recognizing four phases or positions: top (180°), bottom (0°), halfway up (90°) and halfway down (270°) the wave.

Fig. 2-11.   Wave's four phases.

As opposed to the two variables used in frequency shift keying, namely the different tones for signifying ones and zeros, these four phases can be used to signify four different pairs of bits: 00, 11, 10 and 01. These are called *dibits*, and this method of sending data is called *dibit encoded phase shift keying*. It involves a relationship between the previous phase and the present phase, in other words, a *relative* shift.

Actually, two (incompatible) standards for 1200-bps modems exist: Vadic 3400 and AT&T Bell 212A. Both use dibit encoded phase shift keying, but the 212A uses different phase shifts for some of the dibits and also different carrier frequencies.

	Vadic 3400 (developed in 1972)	Bell 212A (developed in 1974)
originate	2250 Hz	1200 Hz
answer	1150 Hz	2400 Hz
dibit 00	90°	90°
01	270°	0°
11	180°	270°
10	0°	180°

Either type of modem sends 1200 bits per second by sending two bits at a time at the rate of 600 dibits per second, meaning that 600 signal changes (baud) per second are on the line with phase shift keying. Using our old formula, we see that (600 baud + 600 baud) × 1.5 Hz equals 1800 Hz, which is still within the phone company's bandwidth.

2400 bps, 600 Baud An even more ingenious method has been worked out for 2400 bps: at 600 baud, two bit pairs at a time are sent. This method is the V.22 bis standard. As previously noted, it was worked out by an international body called the Consultative Committee for International Telegraphy and Telephony (CCITT), which is an advisory committee operating under the United Nations' International Telecommunications Union.

How are two-bit pairs (two dibits or one quadbit) sent at one time? Phase modulation, used for 1200-bps communication, is combined with *amplitude modulation*. Amplitude modulation means that the power level of the signal is varied. For V.22 bis, the two power levels are one unit and three units. The wave form that results from combining this variation in amplitude with phase shifting looks very complex compared to any of the methods discussed previously (amplitude modulation, phase modulation, frequency modulation). The first bit pair is derived from looking at the phase change. The second bit pair is derived from looking at the amplitude change. As in dibit encoded phase shift keying, the signal is compared to the previous signal. The relative shift of phase or change of amplitude determines what the bit pair is. This scheme can be thought of in terms of the quadrants of a circle, with each quadrant containing the four possible bit pairs.

The first pair of bits (from the phase change) selects the quadrant. The second pair (from the amplitude change) selects the dibit within that

Fig. 2-12.   Four quadrants of circle in dibits.

11	10		10	11	
01	00		00	01	
01	00		00	01	
11	10		10	11	

quadrant. For instance, if the first dibit shifts 180° from the previous one, the diagonally opposite quadrant is selected. If the second dibit then shifts 90° from the last dibit received, the next bit pair would be selected, moving counterclockwise within the quadrant.

Fig. 2-13.   Movement of dibits within circle.

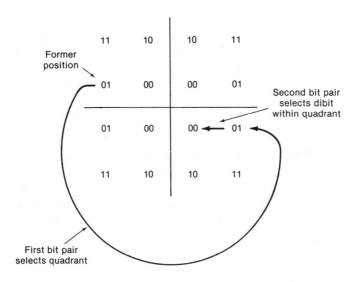

Connecting Equipment

Now look at the equipment in between the modem and the computer: connectors, ports, adapter boards, and cables.

Connectors

Here we're concerned not only with the connectors on the personal computer and on the stand-alone modem but also the connectors at either end of the cable that joins the two. One of the first things people notice about these connectors is that two types seem to exist. They're called *male* and *female*.

Fig. 2-14.   Male connector.

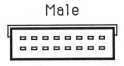

Fig. 2-15.   Female connector.

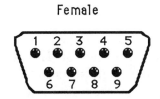

Please note that what determines gender is the *pins* rather than the outer sleeve of the connector. The male connector with pins has an outer sleeve that goes outside the female connector.

Fig. 2-16.   Standard 25-pin connector, male and female.

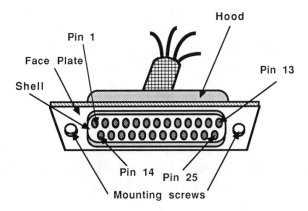

Getting the connectors connected correctly requires paying attention to something besides their genders. The other difference is between Data Terminal Equipment (DTE) and Data Communications Equipment (DCE). The difference has to do with the function of pin 4, called Request to Send (RTS). DTE sends on pin 4 a signal that it wants to send data. DTE receives the signal on its pin 4.

Although you are justified in expecting a modem to be set up as Data Communications Equipment and a computer to be set up as Data Terminal Equipment, exceptions to this rule exist. Chapter 5 details connections for specific computers and modems, answering DTE/DCE questions. In addition, Appendix E describes some equipment that you can use to check connections.

Ports

Port refers to more than the connector. The port is the location through which the computer exchanges information with another piece of equipment. In addition to the hardware interface (the connector), a port has an *address* so that programs know where to send their instructions and data. The two basic types of ports are *serial* and *parallel*. Because modems are serial devices, we are concerned only with serial ports here.

Some computers come with serial ports included. In addition to the male and female 25-pin connectors shown previously, connectors with fewer pins are used. Examples are those connectors used on the Macintosh and the IBM PCjr. Computers that do not include a serial port have some way to let the customer add serial capability. Typically, several internal expansion slots will be available. The IBM PC and the Apple IIe or II+ are prominent examples of machines with expansion slots. These computers get serial capability from asynch plug-in boards with serial connectors that are accessible through the back of the computer.

The UART

Because a modem is a serial device, a modem itself can be an async plug-in board so that no need for a serial connector exists. The modem gets information directly from the computer.

How can this happen, when we all know that the information inside a computer is parallel, conveyed on eight lines or maybe more? The answer is provided by a chip called a universal asynchronous receiver/ transmitter, or UART, (pronounced you-art) for short.

A UART converts parallel data from the computer's bus into serial data that the serial port or device can use. As you might expect, the UART also converts serial data back to parallel data for output to the computer's

SAMS™

Book Mark

Sams books cover a wide range of technical topics. We are always interested in hearing from our readers regarding their informational needs. Please complete this questionnaire and return it to us with your suggestions. We appreciate your comments.

1. Which brand and model of computer do you use?
☐ Apple _____
☐ Commodore _____
☐ IBM _____
☐ Other (please specify) _____
_____

2. Where do you use your computer?
☐ Home   ☐ Work

3. Are you planning to buy a new computer?
☐ Yes   ☐ No
If yes, what brand are you planning to buy? _____

4. Please specify the brand/type of software, operating systems or languages you use.
☐ Word Processing _____
☐ Spreadsheets _____
☐ Data Base Management _____
☐ Integrated Software _____
☐ Operating Systems _____
☐ Computer Languages _____

5. Are you interested in any of the following electronics or technical topics?
☐ Amateur radio
☐ Antennas and propagation
☐ Artificial intelligence/
   expert systems
☐ Audio
☐ Data communications/
   telecommunications
☐ Electronic projects
☐ Instrumentation and measurements
☐ Lasers
☐ Power engineering
☐ Robotics
☐ Satellite receivers

6. Are you interested in servicing and repair of any of the following (please specify)?
☐ VCRs _____
☐ Compact disc players _____
☐ Microwave ovens _____
☐ Television _____
☐ Computers _____
☐ Automotive electronics _____
☐ Mobile telephones _____
☐ Other _____

7. How many computer or electronics books did you buy in the last year?
☐ One or two   ☐ Three or four
☐ Five or six   ☐ More than six

8. What is the average price you paid per book?
☐ Less than $10   ☐ $10-$15
☐ $16-$20   ☐ $21-$25   ☐ $26+

9. What is your occupation?
☐ Manager
☐ Engineer
☐ Technician
☐ Programmer/analyst
☐ Student
☐ Other _____

10. Please specify your educational level.
☐ High school
☐ Technical school
☐ College graduate
☐ Postgraduate

11. Are there specific books you would like to see us publish? _____
_____
_____

Comments _____
_____
_____

Name _____
Address _____
City _____
State/Zip _____

22446

SAMS™

Book Markkram Book

NO POSTAGE
NECESSARY
IF MAILED
IN THE
UNITED STATES

BUSINESS REPLY CARD

FIRST CLASS   PERMIT NO. 1076   INDIANAPOLIS, IND.

POSTAGE WILL BE PAID BY ADDRESSEE

HOWARD W. SAMS & CO., INC.
ATTN: Public Relations Department
P.O. BOX 7092
Indianapolis, IN 46206

SAMS™

bus. A UART or its equivalent is included behind every serial port and on every async board or internal modem.

Some serial devices or interfaces do not have an actual UART chip, but the same functions are provided by other circuitry. A few personal computers have a USART (universal synchronous/asynchronous receiver/transmitter) rather than a UART. The serial card for the Sanyo MBC 555 is an example. Machines with USARTs require special communications software because most programs "expect" to "talk" to a specific UART. However, once you find software to drive USARTs, most stand-alone modems will work with these computers.

The UART adds, subtracts, and interprets the start, stop, and parity bits that we discussed in the section on modems. When the computer has a character to send out, whether seven or eight bits long, the bits goes into an eight-bit buffer in the UART. From there the data bits follows a start bit (zero) into an eleven-bit shift register. The UART then finds out from a controller, either on the modem or in the computer, what the parity bit should be and how many stop bits to add.

When the UART has to deal with incoming data, the character, whether nine, ten, or eleven bits long, goes into an eleven-bit shift register. The start and stop bits are stripped off, and the data bits and parity bit are added. The sum is compared to the parity setting for accuracy. The data bits are sent to an eight-bit buffer, then to the computer.

The UART also contains a control-status section that monitors output pins on the serial connector. When the UART gets a software instruction to change certain output pins from low voltage to high voltage or vice versa, this chip does so.

A UART is included on internal modems that fit into expansion slots in computers. A stand-alone modem does not need to have a UART because one will be behind the serial connector.

Now you know how the (serial) modem talks with the (parallel) computer. If you use software designed to run on your particular computer and drive the modem you have—for instance, software to run on an Apple IIe and drive the Hayes Micromodem—the two devices should be able to talk to each other with no trouble. The software knows how to talk to the serial port or the internal modem.

However, a major exception to this rule is found in the IBM computer family and those computers that are operationally compatible and have more than one expansion slot. Whereas the Apple IIc, for instance, numbers its slots, reserving slot 2 for an internal modem, the IBM PC and its workalikes do not distinguish among the slots in the machine. Therefore, if your computer has an internal modem and another serial board, such as a multifunction board with an asynchronous serial port, how can the computer tell the difference between the two? The user can help. In describing how the user helps, we must bring up the thorny concept of COM (for communication) settings.

COM Settings

COM settings—COM1 and COM2—are *port addresses*, assigned by IBM when it designed the PC. The port address is a number in the section of the computer reserved for I/O. The communications software uses this number to address instructions and data to the board (actually its UART). Both hardware and software have COM settings. These settings must agree in order for hardware and software to work together.

Hardware COM Settings Setting the COM port on modems or other serial boards is accomplished through DIP (dual inline package) switches on these boards. An internal modem probably has only two or three of these small DIP switches, with maybe some added jumper settings. Serial or async boards for the IBM PC may have eight or more DIP switches.

Fig. 2-17.   Hayes board DIP switches.

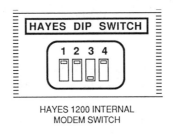

HAYES 1200 INTERNAL
MODEM SWITCH

The manual for the board will tell you how to set the switches. Chapter 5 of this book shows COM settings for leading internal IBM PC modems.

The cardinal rule of COM settings is that each serial device must have its own. If one serial device is set for COM1, a second serial device must be COM2. Most internal serial boards for the IBM PC, including modems, are factory-set for COM1. Recognizing that many PC owners will already have installed another serial device, especially a multifunction board with asynchronous communications, a few modem companies set their modems for COM2.

The IBM PCjr differs from other members of the PC family. This computer has a 16-pin serial connector, set for COM2. COM1 is reserved for the optional 300-bps internal PCjr modem manufactured by IBM.

If you set for COM2 a modem that is the only serial device, the modem will put the COM2 address in the position where COM1 is supposed to appear. This incorrect address can cause trouble. Some communications programs (Smartcom, for one) cannot talk to the modem if the address is not where the program expects it.

Some computers, including the PC itself, allow the user more than two serial devices. Although COM1 and COM2 are predefined by IBM and followed by most of the PC compatibles, COM3 and COM4 do not have preset addresses. Some modems offer COM3, and some offer both COM3 and COM4. The modem or serial board manufacturer chooses addresses from a specific range spelled out in the computer's technical manual.

Software COM Settings   Most sophisticated communications programs, such as PC-TALK, Crosstalk, Smartcom, MITE, GEORGE, and Relay, allow you to set the COM port to agree with the hardware COM port setting. As with modems, the default setting is COM1. An exception is Racal-Vadic's GEORGE, which is set to COM2 like the internal modem with which that program is shipped.

How can you know whether you have COM port incompatibility? Software that runs a diagnostic test on the modem when you boot, like Smartcom, will display a message like "modem not responding". The usual reasons for a modem's unresponsiveness are incorrect cable connectors or a wrong COM port setting. Other software doesn't let you know something is wrong until you try to dial. At that point, the program simply doesn't dial the number you enter or program stops running. If a new modem doesn't work, the second thing to check (after checking all the cables) is the COM setting.

You may have to dig around in the program to find the screen for setting the COM port. This setting is classed with different kinds of parameters, depending on the program. You should have to set the COM port only once. Unless you change modems, the software should use your settings as the new default settings the next time you boot the program.

Software sold with modems that offer COM3 and COM4 has a place for you to set these choices. You specify your choices by entering the port address, which is not predetermined by IBM. The software manual should provide information to help you enter this address.

COM ports are the most troublesome part of installing an internal modem in the IBM PC. Most of the problems that new users have are COM port incompatibilities, according to modem manufacturers in this market. Please note that the COM port problem can occur with stand-alone modems plugged in a serial adapter board if the computer is a PC or compatible that uses this same scheme of unnumbered slots. A serial adapter board is usually factory-set for COM1.

Version 2.1 MS-DOS and PC-DOS system disks include a program called MODE.COM, which sets modes of operation for the printer, the monitor, and the asynchronous communications adapter. This program offers a choice between COM1 and COM2 and also other communications settings such as speed, parity, and number of stop bits and data bits. This program works in conjunction with a BASIC program called COMM.BAS, which includes terminal emulation and proper data format settings for the major online services (information utilities).

Adapter Boards

Serial adapter boards, *asynchronous adapter boards*, and *asynchronous boards* are equivalent names for the plug-in boards mentioned in the discussion of serial connectors. Boards are designed to fit inside specific computers. Sometimes adapter boards are small units, properly called cards rather than boards.

In addition to boards that provide only serial capability, *multifunction boards* are also available. These can offer memory expansion, a clock with battery backup, as well as the serial interface. On some boards the serial interface can be changed to a parallel port by setting DIP switches. Boards with two ports are available also.

Serial boards are usually factory-set for COM1. This setting can be changed by flipping one or two DIP switches, closely following directions in the board's user manual. If you do find it necessary to reset your async board to COM2, make sure your communications program is also set to COM2.

Cables

For stand-alone modems, the cable is the crux of the matter. The cable that connects your modem to the serial connector on the computer (or async board) had better be right. If you want to make your own cable, you must be absolutely sure that every lead is correct. Mistakes here can have dramatic results.

Chapter 5 details cable connections for each major computer-modem combination. These connections have been tested and many are available commercially. Appendix E describes equipment that is useful in constructing your own cables. Appendix F shows what you need to know for soldering and such.

3

A Call's Progress

As a first step in understanding how a modem and a computer interact, let's review the differences between Data Terminal Equipment (DTE) and Data Communications Equipment (DCE), as defined by the Electronic Industry Association's Recommended Standard 232, revision C. The most important difference lies in the function of pin 4, Request to Send (RTS): DTE signals that it wants to send data to the DCE.

Another classic difference between DTE and DCE lies on the pins of the RS-232-C interface on which each sends and receives data: A DTE sends on pin 2 and receives on pin 3, and a DCE sends on pin 3 and receives on pin 2. However, these pins are sometimes switched. RTS, on the other hand, always goes from DCE to DTE.

The RS-232 Connector

The RS-232-C interface usually appears in the form of a D-shaped connector with 25 pins or sockets, called a DB-25 connector. However, not all DB-25 connectors should be presumed to be RS-232-C connectors. Parallel interfaces and non-RS-232-C interfaces also use this connector. Furthermore, not all RS-232-C interfaces use the DB-25 connector. Examples of computers with fewer than 25 pins in this connector are the Macintosh and the IBM PC jr. As we shall see, modem-computer communication by no means requires all 25 pins.

Can you look at a connector and tell whether a given computer or modem is DTE or DCE? Not really. DCE is usually female, but DTE can be either sex. Put another way, female connectors are almost always DCE. Male connectors could be either DCE or DTE. You also can't presume that computers will be DTE or even that modems will be DCE.

In this book we classify the RS-232-C connector on each computer that has one. The stand-alone modems described in this book are all

RS-232-C. We classify the modems as to whether they are DTE or DCE.

Now, look at the pins on the RS-232-C interface used for modem-computer communication.

Table 3-1.   Pins Used for Data Transmission

Pin No.	Abbreviation	Explanation
Pin 2	TXD	Transmitted Data. DTE ♦ DCE. The DTE transmits TD data to the DCE on this pin.
Pin 3	RXD	Received Data. DTE ♦ DCE. The DTE receives data RD on this pin from the DCE.

Pins 2 and 3 are an input-output pair.

Table 3-2.   Pins Used for Control

Pin No.	Abbreviation	Explanation
Pin 4	RTS	Request to Send. DTE ♦ DCE. The DTE signals that it is ready to send data to DCE.
Pin 5	CTS	Clear to Send. DTE ♦ DCE. The DCE signals that it is ready to accept data from the DTE. In full duplex communication, pin 5 always goes high after handshaking is complete (pin 8 has gone high). Also used to control the flow of data. Most flow control is effected in software these days.
Pin 6	DSR	Data Set Ready. DTE ♦ DCE. The DCE (Data Set = modem) signals that it is connected to the phone line.
Pin 8	CXR DCD RLSD	Data Carrier Detect (originally named Received Line Signal Detect in the RSZ-32-C standard). DTE ♦ DCE. Modem tells computer that modem has gone online and terminal can receive data. When this input is *disabled*, no more data is received from the DCE.
Pin 12	SI	Speed Indicator. DTE ♦ DCE. The DCE tells the DTE whether the modem is in low or high speed. Used by many modem manufacturers, although this use of pin 12 is not strictly RS-232-C standard.

Table 3-2.—cont.   Pins Used for Control

Pin No.	Abbreviation	Explanation
Pin 20	DTR	Data Terminal Ready. DTE ♦ DCE. The DTE signals that it is powered up and ready. Controls auto answer, auto originate.
Pin 22	RI	Ring Indicator. DTE ♦ DCE. The modem tells the computer that ring voltage is coming in.

Table 3-3.   Pins Not Used for Data or for Control

Pin No.	Abbreviation	Explanation
Pin 1	GND	Protective Frame Ground.
Pin 7	SG	Signal Ground, Common, Signal Common. DTE ♦ ♦ DCE. The reference point for all other voltages in the interface. Pin 7 is not a frame ground as pin 1 is. Pin 7 is always connected. Pins 1 and 7 may be connected to each other internally.

For summary, see Figure 3-1.

Fig. 3-1.   Modem-computer communication summary.

```
DTE                      DCE
GND    1 ———————— 1  GND   Frame Ground
TXD    2 ————————→ 2  TXD   Transmitted Data
RXD    3 ←———————— 3  RXD   Received Data
RTS    4 ————————→ 4  RTS   Request to Send
CTS    5 ←———————— 5  CTS   Clean to Send
DSR    6 ←———————— 6  DSR   Data Set Ready
SG     7 ———————— 7  SG    Signal Common, Signal Ground
CXR    8 ←———————— 8  CXR   Carrier Detect
SI    12 ←————————12  SI    Speed Indicator
DTR   20 ————————→20  DTR   Data Terminal Ready
RI    22 ←————————22  RI    Ring Indicator
```

The Progress of a Call

When you pick up the telephone receiver and the phone goes *offhook*, a switch or relay is closed in your telephone (*telset* to use the telephone company's term). You may hear a delicate click from inside the modem as the relay—an electrically operated switch—closes. This process corresponds to what happens when you lift the telephone receiver (subset). The only differences between this relay and its nineteenth-century ancestors are in size and power consumption, both much reduced. In a modem, the relay is surrounded by a great deal of advanced electronics.

Once the relay closes, your computer is connected to the telephone systems. At this point, pin 6, DSR, goes high: the modem is telling the computer that it is connected to the line.

The dial tone may be conveyed to you, the user, by the modem's speaker. Alternatively, you may be informed of the dial tone by a communications program that interprets a signal the modem gives. This signal tells the program that the voltage for dial tone is coming in. You are informed of the absence of a dial tone through the same methods.

If an autodial modem is placing the call, the *dialer* portion of this modem dials the number that the computer's keyboard or memory makes available. The autodial feature has become so cheap that most of the modems for small computers are autodial modems these days. If, however, the modem is a manual modem, a human must dial the number in the traditional way: on a telephone handset connected to the modem.

Next, the phone number being dialed is supposed to respond with a *ringback* signal. You may well have presumed all these years that you hear the actual phone on the other end ring when you call somebody, but what you really hear is the ringback signal sent by the central office (exchange) of the number you are calling. A modem with a speaker will broadcast the ringback signal. A modem not using a speaker has a ringback detector, which looks for a particular pattern of frequencies on the telephone line and tells the computer that the other end is ringing. (If the ring pattern differs from the usual ring pattern, which in the United States is a ring lasting 2 seconds, a pause of 4 seconds, a ring lasting 2 seconds, a pause of 4 seconds, and so on, the modem may have trouble detecting the ring.)

What if the other phone responds with a busy signal? Modems with speakers merely broadcast the sound. The modem's circuitry outputs a message to the screen or to communications software to alert the user that the number is busy. A modem not using a speaker usually is able to detect the frequency for the busy signal. The modem tells the communication software, which puts a message on screen for the user.

Pin 20, Data Terminal Ready, is already high, which happened when the computer entered terminal mode, detected the presence of a modem (communications program polled the interface or COM port), or was caused by a default setting in the communications program. Pin 4, the computer's Request to Send, came up with DTR.

When the ringing stops (the link is completed), handshake and carrier detect occur. Before we look at these processes, though, look what has been happening at the other end of the telephone link.

The Answering Modem

When the ring voltage reaches a modem set up in answer mode, pin 22, Ring Indicator, goes high to inform the computer of the incoming call. If DTR is present (pin 20 is high), the modem causes the line relay to close and the ringing stops. When this happens, pin 6, Data Set Ready, goes high, and the modem tells the computer that the modem is connected to the telephone line and is going into handshaking.

The Handshake

Both modems are now offhook, but they aren't yet *online*. The answering modem sends its answer tone. The frequency of the answer tone depends on the kind of modem being used.

Bell 103 (300 bps): 2225 Hz

Bell 212A (1200 bps): 2225 Hz

Racal-Vadic 3400 (0-300, 1200 bps): 2225 Hz or 2025 Hz

Note: the idle condition is MARK (= 1).

The originating modem then sends *its* tone:

Bell 103 (300 bps): 1270 Hz (the idle condition is MARK)

Bell 212A (1200 bps): 1200 Hz (carrier)

Racal-Vadic 3400 (1200 bps): 2250 Hz (carrier)

Whether the originating modem sends 1270, 1200, or 2250 Hz determines whether communication follows the Bell 103, Bell 212A, or Vadic 3400 standard, setting, among other things, the speed at either 300 or 1200 bps.

The originating modem's pin 8, CXR, carrier detect, now goes high and stays high as long as the originating modem detects the appropriate tone from the answering modem. CXR indicates to the computer that the answering modem is online. The computer can now receive on pin 3. A few milliseconds after the sending modem detects the special frequency put out by the answering modem, the sending modem's pin 5, CTS, goes high, indicating that the computer is ready for data.

When the answering modem detects the sending modem's tone, the answering modem's pin 8, CXR, goes high, telling the computer that the modem is online and ready to receive data. CXR stays high as long as a tone is detected from the other end, which brings up CTS, pin 5 and lets the computer know the sending modem is ready to send data out through the line.

Carrier

The term *carrier* properly applies only to a 1200-bps modem, such as 212A, Vadic 3400, or faster modems. These modems use a single frequency modulated to transmit 1s and 0s. The modems send two bits with each phase change (phase shift keying). The 300-bps Bell 103 modems, on the other hand, signal the difference between 1s and 0s by sending different frequencies (see Chapter 2).

Disconnecting

Disconnecting can happen any of several ways, depending on the modem, the software, and the condition of the phone line.

A software instruction can cause pin 20 to go low, disconnecting the modem from the phone line. The modem resets itself to idle, and pin 8 (carrier) drops. Software using Hayes (AT) protocol can send a command (+ + +) that returns the modem to command mode. Another command (ATH) opens the relay. Software using the Vadic protocol sends CTRL C CTRL D to open the relay.

A disturbance on the phone line can interrupt the frequency, causing pin 8 to go low.

A break key on a terminal or a software instruction that imitates this key can send a *continuous space* or a space lasting several character times, which causes Bell 103 and 212A modems to disconnect.

Summary

Here is a summary of the sequence of events.

Table 3-4.   Event Summary

	Originating Modem	Answering Modem
1	Pin 4 RTS Computer signals that it wishes to send data to modem.	Pin 4 RTS Computer signals that it wishes to send data to modem.
2	Pin 20 DTR Computer signals that it is powered up.	Pin 20 DTR Computer signals that it is powered up.
3	Modem goes offhook. Dial tone received.	
4	Pin 6 DSR (line relay closed) Modem signals that it is connected to the line.	
5	Dials answering modem's number.	Ring voltage is generated.
6	Modem detects ringback signal from answering modem.	Pin 22 RI Modem tells computer that ring is incoming. Goes offhook.
7		Pin 6 DSR Modem signals that it is con- nected to the line.
	The Handshake	
8		Modem sends answer tone.
9	Modem sends mark frequency or carrier, depending on speed selected.	
10		Modem answer tone adjusts to speed of originating modem, if possible.

Table 3-4.—cont.   Event Summary

The Handshake—cont.

Note: In the international standard (which includes 2400 bps transmission) V.22 bis operation, the calling modem adjusts to the speed of the answering modem.

11	Pin 8 CXR Modem signals that it is online.	Pin 8 CXR Modem signals that it is online.
12	Pin 5 CTS Modem signals that it is ready for data.	Pin 5 CTS Modem signals that it is ready for data.

Data Transmission

Pin 2 TXD Computer transmits data.	Pin 2 TXD Computer transmits data.
Pin 3 RXD Computer receives data.	Pin 3 RXD Computer receives data.

Full Duplex and Half Duplex Mode

Major modems for personal computers, such as the modems discussed in this book, are full duplex. These modems are capable of sending and receiving at the same time, as we saw in Chapter 2. Half duplex modems, by contrast, can send in both directions, but only one way at a time. These modems use a slightly different handshake at the beginning of communication. More handshaking is required when the line is turned around (the modem equivalent of "over to you").

You will see settings in many communications programs for choosing between full duplex and half duplex. This setting does not mean that these modems can alternate between full duplex and half duplex operation. Rather, the setting means that some confusion exists about one of the features associated with half duplex: *local echo*, also known as *local copy*.

The confusion arises because the original terminals, which were teletype machines, were essentially printers. These machines had a button for local copy so that operators could see what they were sending. Communications between these terminals and mainframe computers were half duplex. Thus local echo or local copy is not an inherent quality of half duplex communication but is associated with it.

In full duplex operation, the mainframe sends characters back as an error check. This remote echo is not an inherent quality of full duplex operation but is associated with it.

The choice *half duplex (mode, operation)* in a communications program simply means *local echo*, which exists for communicating with systems that will not send, for whatever reason, your characters back to your screen. Modems and terminals with a hardware switch for local echo also are available.

4

Communications Software

A modem is a sleek little device. Most modems for small computers do not have any knobs or buttons, just a few indicator lights at most. How then do you tell a modem what to do? You use communications software. Software is the link between your computer and your modem.

If you have an internal modem, the modem company probably included software. Because an internal modem is designed to work with a particular personal computer, the software that the modem company so generously wrote or selected for you will run on that computer.

If you have a stand-alone modem, however, you are in the market for communications software. Stand-alone modems can work with a variety of computers, given the right cable. Because the modem manufacturers cannot guess whether you are going to need a communications program that will work with the operating system of an Apple IIe, a Macintosh, an IBM PC or a Commodore, they wisely let you try to find your own communications software.

You are also in the market for communications software if you have an internal modem but are not satisfied with the software that was included. Of all the different categories of personal computer software on the market today, few come in for a bigger share of complaints than communications software. Because relatively few people have been using modems with personal computers so far, all the refinements and thoughtful touches you have come to expect in other types of software have yet to occur to most of the people who design communications software. In addition, the field of telecommunications bristles with technical terms you won't find anywhere else. Compounding this problem is the fact that some of this jargon is misused by people in the field.

Types of Communications Programs

A typical computer store carries two or three communications programs that dominate the market, programs with list prices in the $100-$200 range. If you do some research, you may discover other programs that seem preferable within the second rank of commercially available software, ranging in price from $80 to $200. In addition, one or two communications programs are "marketed" under the Freeware™ concept, and programs varying from free to cheap are available from user groups and bulletin boards. Start at the low end.

You still can get the descendants of the first communications programs from user groups and from bulletin boards. Be warned, however, that these public domain programs are not for the novice. Furthermore, they don't include many labor-saving features.

Another way of saving money on communications software is to cobble up a *terminal emulation program* in BASIC yourself. Computer magazines run listings of these programs every once in a while. A terminal emulation program sets up your computer to act like a dumb terminal (as if it had no innate intelligence but were being directed by a powerful computer elsewhere). Once your machine is in terminal mode, you can enter commands directly to your modem. You will find the commands for your modem in the documentation that came with the modem. If you have an IBM PC, your PC-DOS disk includes a simple BASIC program called COMM.BAS. It won't dial because IBM has no way of knowing what modem you'll get for your PC, but COMM.BAS has the proper data configuration for the major online services.

If you want more than you can get out of a bare-bones program from a user group or a program you write, commercial and semicommercial software producers have striven to meet your needs. These producers offer a broad spectrum of programs, ranging in price, as we have seen, from $35 (Shareware or Freeware) to $200, needing as little memory as 64K or as much as 192K, with features ranging from the bare minimum all the way up to programmability and electronic mail. In terms of ease of use, much more uniformity exists: communications software producers are gradually responding to users' cries of pain and frustration, and the stuff is getting better.

Features

Following are some of the main features that you can reasonably expect from a communications program, grouped by function and in rough order of importance.

Call Placement from Keyboard

If you have an autodial modem that can dial a number you enter from your computer's keyboard, the communications program you choose should take advantage of that feature by allowing you to type in the telephone number on the keyboard.

Call Progress Information

Many modems for personal computers have speakers. (Some modems with speakers have a volume control for users who don't want to listen to the amplified sound of the telephone company's buzzes and squawks.) A few other modems can be connected to the computer's speaker to accomplish the same purpose. Typically, these modems can detect only a limited number of the signals from the phone line and simply let you listen to the sounds.

Modems that don't have an onboard speaker usually have the intelligence to detect call progress signals from the phone line, such as ringing, busy, and answer tone. If you have one of these modems, your software should be able to show you this call progress information by displaying call progress messages, such as **ringing**, **answer tone received**, **busy**. The program also should let you know when a telephone signal is missing—for example, *no dial tone*. If you want software with call progress messages to drive your speakerless modem, the best source is that modem's manufacturer. The company probably produces its own program or can recommend one.

Telephone Directory

Most sophisticated communications programs offer some form of directory. Programs vary widely in terms of the number of entries the software holds, how convenient it is to use, how easy it is to set up, and what settings can be attached to a telephone number. Some directories that offer many features turn out to be cumbersome to use. If possible, try before you buy.

As you enter a telephone number into the directory, most programs assign a letter of the alphabet or a number to that directory entry, which is how you select that entry to place a call. A few programs let you choose your own descriptive names for directory entries.

In most programs, you can store useful settings related to each telephone number—speed (300, 1200, 2400 bps), number of data bits used by that system, and so on. These settings automatically go into effect when the number is dialed. You also may be able to store your user ID and password to that number or even several text strings that are automatically sent in response to questions from the remote system. It is "terribly" elegant to punch in a directory entry, then sit on your hands while the program logs on and gets all the way down to the specialized part of the system in which you are interested.

Some programs also let you store *redial information* for each telephone number. You may be able to store the number of times each number should be redialed if busy and to specify the amount of time between retries.

Just to confuse the issue, some personal computer modems have enough memory space of their own to store a few telephone numbers. Sometimes this storage includes redial information and a log-on sequence.

Answer Capability and Security

Most modems for the personal computer market can answer calls as well as make them, so commercial software sets your modem to answer calls. Unattended answer capability is the key to a simple electronic mail system. A personal computer in a home office, for instance, can serve as the company "mainframe" so that employees in the field can send reports to the computer and receive updates and instructions.

Unattended answer unfortunately can appeal to some creative individual who zaps everything on the company hard disk, substitutes data, overwrites files with other files that contain worms, or perpetrates other charming practical jokes. Security, therefore, becomes important in this kind of system.

In regular all-purpose programs, one password level is the only protection the answering system has. More sophisticated (and expensive) programs primarily designed for electronic mail offer at least two password levels and ways of protecting individual files. Another security feature to look for is an *audit trail* that records each caller's activity (keystrokes). Some modems incorporate powerful security features in their firmware (onboard read-only software). Security features will probably burgeon along with the modem market.

Another whiz-bang feature that sometimes is available with unattended answer is *attention message* capability. Callers with problems or questions send a short message that appears on the unattended screen and is accompanied by a few beeps to alert any human who happens to be around at the receiving end.

Voice/Data Switching

Suppose that you are a user with one computer, one modem, and one telephone line, and you want to exchange material with another user who has the same setup. You have to call that person to let him or her know what your plan is. The two of you may have to work out such details as transmission speed, parity, and the number of data bits and stop bits. After your telephone conversation, you may feel that your system is very low-tech if you have to redial the same number with your modem. To avoid this awkwardness, some modems let you switch from voice (human-to-human) to data (computer-to-computer) communication on the same phone call and back again if you want. Not all modems are capable of voice/data switching. If your modem is capable of such switching, use software supplied by your modem company or its recommended program.

Redialing

Some programs allow redialing only after a busy signal. Others allow redialing the last number dialed regardless of what has happened in the meantime. Redialing only after a busy signal uses fewer keystrokes but is restrictive. Redialing the last number dialed any time you want usually requires getting back to a certain point in the program, which will almost always take a few keystrokes.

With some programs you can set the number of retries per phone number and the interval between retries. These software packages let you store this information individually for each number in your directory.

Chain Dialing

A few programs let you chain directory entries so that if one number is busy, the modem automatically dials the next one until you finally get through to a telephone number on your list. Retries can be built into this setup if the program lets you set the number of retries for each telephone directory entry.

Calling through a list of numbers is a key electronic mail feature, like unattended answer. For electronic mail, though, you want your program to reach every number on the list rather than call numbers until one is reached. If designed for electronic mail, the program lets you send a message, perhaps send files under an error-checking protocol, and get messages or files from the numbers the program calls.

Unattended Dialing

Unattended dialing is much more complex than unattended answer. Only the most sophisticated of the big programs (more than $100) offer this kind of dialing. It lets you select a phone number and specify a later time for the program to place the call, which means that your system can, for example, find out how your stocks are doing without your having to be at your computer. Unattended dialing means that you can send your report to the main office after eleven p.m. when the rates go down and maybe have your system ask the home office computer for updates and instructions as well. Obviously, such a program also needs the capability of capturing incoming material that results from the calls the program makes. Files are not usually a problem (using an error-checking protocol). Some programs will make a file out of incoming material that is not in file form. Other programs will print the material while it is coming in.

File Transfer

A communications program should allow you to send and receive files with an appropriate degree of accuracy. Simple ASCII text files are one thing: Tragedy does not occur if here and there one letter gets dropped or changed into another because of noise on the phone line. But if you are sending a program, a binary file, or even an ASCII text with sensitive information, such as a group of figures, you do not want a single character to be corrupted. How can you ensure the integrity of a transmission that uses the regular phone lines? One way of protecting files as you send them into the switched network is to use an *error-checking protocol*.

A protocol is simply an agreed-on set of rules. In personal computer communications, two kinds of protocols are important: the dialing protocol and the data transfer protocol. People tend to get these protocols confused.

Dialing Protocol

The *dialing protocol* governs the way the computer sends commands to the modem. An example is the Hayes dialing protocol, developed by Hayes Microcomputer Corp. (then known as D.C. Hayes) and now used by a lot of hardware and software manufacturers pursuing "Hayes compatibility" (another misused term that means something different to each manufacturer). Typically, the Hayes modems and Hayes "compatible" modems are programmed to accept certain commands, all preceded by AT (for attention). ATD tells the Hayes modem to dial the number that follows, ATDT tells this modem to use tone dialing rather than pulse and so on. Problems typically arise when the unsuspecting user runs software designed not only for the Hayes command set but also for the Hayes timing sequences. Not all Hayes command compatible modems are timing compatible.

If you are using software that drives a Hayes or Hayes compatible modem, the software probably won't require you to remember these letters. For example, Hayes' own software, Smartcom, requires you to choose number 1 on its menu if you want to place a call, then select 0 for originate versus A for answer, before you enter the telephone directory entry you want dialed.

Data Transfer Protocols

The other important type of protocol, the *data transfer protocol*, governs how data is sent and received. Many data transfer protocols exist. Following are the most popular.

The *XMODEM* protocol started out being used for file transfer in the bulletin-board world where this protocol now dominates. It has spread to at least one major online service. All communications programs that hope for any share of the market now include XMODEM.

Worth noting is the fact that this standard, one of the few in the field of personal computer communications, was not imposed from above by a big company but came from users. XMODEM was devised in 1977 by a computer professional named Ward Christensen. He wanted to transfer programs written by other people to a noncompatible system, his 20K Altair kit, using then innovative floppy disks. Because he also was one of the people who set up the first bulletin board, use of his XMODEM protocol spread along with the use of bulletin boards.

XMODEM sets the data word at eight data bits, no parity, and one stop bit. XMODEM has been ported from the original CP/M operating system version to PC-DOS, MS-DOS, and Macintosh. An enhanced version of XMODEM allows transmission of batches of files. Although the traditional versions use *longitudinal redundancy checking*, a version using *cyclic redundancy checking* (CRC-16) also exists. Following text in this chapter describes how these types of error checking work.

XMODEM operates in half duplex, with the sender waiting for an acknowledgment from the receiver before sending the next block. This acknowledgment is not error-protected. If the checksums do not agree, XMODEM automatically retransmits the data. XMODEM is considered to afford more than 97 percent accuracy for data transmission.

Kermit, a free but non-public-domain (meaning Kermit cannot be sold for profit) protocol, was developed at Columbia University, which uses the frog's name by permission. Kermit has been adapted to virtually any microcomputer you can think of, as well as minicomputers and mainframes. Some versions of Kermit are more than an error-checking protocol. They are communications programs, including terminal emulation and other major features. Kermit for PC-DOS or MS-DOS allows a choice of longitudinal redundancy checking (like XMODEM) or cyclic redundancy checking. Some versions allow the user to choose between seven and eight data bits and one or two stop bits.

MNP or Microcom Networking Protocol was developed by Microcom, Inc., which licenses this protocol to other companies. It has full duplex communication and that means less time on overhead—important for 2400-bps transmission. MNP uses cyclic redundancy checking, which has proved much more reliable as an error-checking method, especially for 2400-bps communication, than longitudinal redundancy checking. MNP is capable of synchronous transmission with no start and stop bits. This protocol allows both sides of the data link to determine if switching to synchronous transmission is possible.

MNP is vying with X.PC, another protocol using cyclic redundancy checking, to replace XMODEM as the standard microcomputer data transfer protocol. MNP versions have been created for Apple and Tandy computers and the IBM PC family. MNP has been incorporated into services like MCI Mail, British Telecom, and GTE Telenet. Software companies, like Lotus Development, Visicorp, and Dow Jones, have licensed MNP. To implement MNP as a chip on a modem is advantageous. Many modem companies have licensed MNP even if they haven't implemented it.

X.PC was developed by Tymnet from the CCITT's X.25 data transfer protocol, used in wide-area networks (mainframes-to-micro data communications networks). The Tymnet data network (part of Tymnet-McDonnell Douglas) distributes information on X.PC to interested vendors. If they decide to incorporate X.PC, Tymnet sends to them the source and driver code written in Lattice C.

Like X.25, X.PC provides networking capability. X.PC can handle 15 simultaneous channels on the same line, allowing the user to communicate with up to eight hosts, and is especially suited to use with windowing software. X.PC is capable of synchronous transmission as well as asynchronous. Besides Tymnet itself, MCI Mail, MicroSoft, and Concord Data Systems are incorporating X.PC.

Error Checking

Data transfer protocols generally perform a mathematical computation on some unit of the data and transmit the result of the computation, which is called a *checksum*, along with the unit of data. The receiving end performs the same computation and compares its checksum with the one received. If a discrepancy occurs, the unit of data may or may not be retransmitted. The three main methods of error checking have their own kinds of checksum.

Vertical redundancy checking involves using a parity bit. (See Chapter 2 for an explanation of this term.) In this method, the data bits of each character are summed. For even parity, a one or zero is appended to make an even total. For odd parity, a one or zero is appended to make an odd total. Vertical redundancy checking can detect only an odd number of bit errors. Of course, the parity bit itself can be in error. Parity schemes do not usually include resending the character.

Longitudinal redundancy checking performs its computations on a *block* of characters rather than on each character. XMODEM sets blocks of 128 bytes. It adds the bits in the start of header character, the block number, the block number two's complement (or one's complement), and the 128 bytes in the block to produce its checksum. This method is considered to be more than 97 percent accurate in indicating errors. Protocols using longitudinal redundancy checking usually include retransmission of faulty data blocks (XMODEM, Kermit).

Cyclic redundancy checking performs more complex mathematics on the block of data. The schemes most often used are CRC-15 (the CCITT's V.41) and CRC-16. CRC-16 is considered more accurate. These methods, which include retransmission of faulty data blocks, are widely used in synchronous communication.

Both CRC-16 and CRC-15 add the bits in a block of data, expressing the sum as a binary number. This number is divided in a certain way by another predetermined binary number called the *generator polynomial* $x^{16} + x^{15} + x^2 + 1$ for CRC-16 and $x^{15} + x^8 + x^5 + 1$ for CRC-15). The remainder, expressed in sixteen bits, becomes the checksum, appended to the block of data. CRC-16 can detect all odd numbers of error bits, all single error bursts up to sixteen bits, 99.9969 percent of all possible single error bursts of seventeen bits, and 99.9984 percent of all error bursts longer than seventeen bits.

Control Character Problems

Some files contain *control characters*. Word-processing files often contain quite a variety of these characters. The problem with control characters is that different systems—computers, software, online services—use these characters for different functions. Do not look for much standardization here, because implementation of these very different needs cannot be standardized.

Communications software deals in different ways with control characters: stripping them (some if not all), displaying them, converting them. Some programs allow the user some control over what happens to control characters.

Dealing with Nonfile Material

Most programs let you save incoming material that is not in file form, such as all the up-to-the-minute stuff from an online service. However, you may have to set up a capture file in advance, which can be awkward if you do not plan ahead (and who does?). The program may not allow you to switch material to a different drive while your modem is online.

Printing

Practically all communications programs allow printing as your system receives the material. Some programs have special settings for the printer (initialization string) besides the usual one, which lets you set the number of null characters. Null characters carry no meaning but allow a little time for a print head to return to the left margin of the paper.

Adaptability

Most programs allow you to change settings, such as transmission speed, number of data bits, number of stop bits, parity, local echo on/off, and line feed with or without carriage return. Because settings obviously are not standardized, you have to find out what settings the other system uses by trial and error, unless that system is a large one with requirements which you can look up. You should be able to change settings without having to hang up.

Displays and Other Help Features

Some programs, especially those produced by modem manufacturers to work with their products, run tests on the modem as soon as you boot. More or less helpful error messages appear if something does not check out.

Communications programs should display connect status messages, such as **connected**, **online**, and **offline**. Many programs display the elapsed time during a call to help you keep track of how much money is disappearing through the telephone line. When you are not connected, the place on the screen for elapsed time is usually occupied by the present time and date in these programs.

For file transfer, getting easily to your file directory (preferably in alphabetized format) is important. The usefulness of the file directory is greatly enhanced if the size of each file is displayed. Some programs also display what amount of time at the current speed setting is necessary to send the file, for instance:

Mystuff.txt   36K   24 min

In addition, a program may tell you how much space is left on the disk drive to which the computer is logged. After a file is transferred, some programs display how many bytes were received.

Onscreen help in communications software is pretty standard. Off-screen help, in the form of a user manual, should have a variety of examples as well as straightforward explanations of the program's commands, menus, and functions. A troubleshooting section is comforting when you are getting used to all the new stuff. Manuals are easier to use if they have tabs and a comprehensive index. The software producers are responding to users' requests and complaints in this department.

Text Strings, Command Files, Programming

The ability to store a text string (such as your user ID, password, and/or name) to a function key is fairly standard, even in simple programs. Command files, which tell the modem to call a certain number, log on for you, and get you down several layers into a system—all on one command — are offered by the big programs. At least one also offers branching, which allows the program to make choices. Using these options may require learning a special programming language included in the software. A nice compromise is programmability that doesn't require learning a programming language. One possibility is recording keystrokes, then executing them on command. When you call up a communications program that offers programability you can usually add the name of one of your programs so that your program is automatically executed.

Editor

A little text editor for dashing off messages you are about to send can be a convenience, eliminating the need to switch to your word-processing program. However, you might find inconvenient having to learn another bunch of complicated word-processing commands just to type a few lines.

Ease of Use

Ease of use is the great intangible, unquantifiable, unclassifiable of software and after function (what the program actually does) a program's second most important characteristic. Fancy features won't matter much if you discover that dialing a number takes five keystrokes every time. Try before you buy.

Any software should display onscreen the commands for getting back to the main menu, getting out of the program, or stopping whatever process is in progress. The only thing worse than feeling you can't get out of a situation is feeling you can't get out of a situation that is costing money. In communications software, the user shouldn't have to memorize the commands necessary to hang up the phone. They belong onscreen.

Ease of Learning

Ease of learning has to do with the jargon quotient. A leading communications program thrusts a screenful of technical terms at the user, mixing commands that are rarely used with important ones like those that select transmission speed and buries the command for dialing a number. Figuring out how to place a call can take a new user hours. Does communications software have to be like this?

Now that you know what some communications programs offer, how can you find the one you need?

If you are thinking of acquiring a communications program, look at how much memory the program requires before you do anything else. Also, make sure it comes in a version for your computer. If the program is commercially distributed, find a store that carries the program and ask to see a demonstration. If the program is Freeware, contact another user or the manufacturer for a copy. Ask user groups and read reviews to gain more information about the program you are considering.

The main thing you have to do is what you did when you bought your computer: You figured out what you were going to use it for, then got the machine and software that fit your needs. The following are some chief uses for personal computer communications.

Uses

Online Services

If you are going to be using your modem for getting information on stocks, airline schedules, wire service news and the like from The Source, Dow Jones, or CompuServe, you need software that can connect you to your favorite service with a minimum of fuss—one keystroke is about right. This means programming capability or at least a directory that is accessible right after you boot up the program. It is elegant to have your user ID and password transmitted automatically in response to the prompts from the online service and even neater if the commands to get to the part of the service you are interested in also are automatic. You may want a way to save the material you get from the service, or you may want to print the material as it comes in. Unattended operation comes in handy, for example, if you want to catch up on your stocks at a certain time every day whether or not you are at your computer.

Some of the major communications programs already have directory entries for the major online services, complete with all the proper settings (number of data bits and so on). A few offer subheadings so that you can get to a specific part of an online service. For instance, under the directory entry for The Source will be a collection of routines with the commands for getting directly to the airline schedule, the UPI newswire, market quotes, or your own mailbox.

Public Bulletin Boards

Calling *public bulletin boards* (BBS) differs from calling online services in that free bulletin boards are much harder to get on. They typically have only one telephone line. A program that redials a busy number for as many times as you want at intervals you specify will help you here. Instead of trying to get through to one board, you may want to try several. In that case, a feature that lets you set up a list of numbers to dial through becomes the thing to have.

If you are trying out new bulletin boards, you definitely want a program that lets you change parameters like speed, line feed with or without carriage return and local echo on/off, because bulletin boards vary. You should be able to change these settings without hanging up because days may go by before you can get back on a popular board. Once you have gotten on a system and know what settings it requires, your program should let you store this information to the phone number, along with your user ID and password.

If you want to download the wonderful free software available on some bulletin boards, you need the XMODEM protocol.

Company Communication

If you are going to be calling *another personal computer* in your company and sending or receiving reports or files, look for unattended calling features and an error-checking protocol. Of course, you probably want the same program to run on the computer in the office, so you want unattended answer and some form of security.

If you are going to be communicating with a *mainframe* in your company, you may have problems with control characters. Find a program that allows you to set what is filtered or converted. If you do not know what characters might be causing problems, a program that displays all characters or has a debug feature is useful.

If you are sending WordStar files to a person who will need to look at the file in WordStar on his or her end, an error-checking protocol like XMODEM or Kermit is usually sufficient to guard against control characters being garbled. For a while, one of the leading communications programs used an error-checking protocol that added characters to WordStar files which rendered them uneditable. Eventually the manufacturer added the XMODEM protocol to its program.

5
Charts and Drawings

In this chapter, you will find charts for connecting each of the modems and computers listed in Table 5-1.

Table 5-1.   Modems & Computers for Which Charts Are Provided

Modems	Computers
Hayes Smartmodem 1200	Apple IIc
Novation Smart-Cat	Apple IIe
Prometheus ProModem 1200	Apple Macintosh
Racal-Vadic 212PA	IBM-PC and XT
Racal-Vadic 1200V	IBM-PC AT
Racal-Vadic 2400PA	IBM-PC jr
Racal-Vadic 2400V	Morrow MD3-P
Racal-Vadic 3451	Osborne
U.S. Robotics Password	Seequa Chameleon
Volksmodem 12	

The modems and computers listed in Table 5-2 do not have specific charts to diagram their connection, but by reference to the appropriate chart identified in the Jump Table, you can find the information that you need.

Table 5-2.   Modems & Computers for Which Jump Table Specifies Chart

Modems	Computers
Cermetek	AT&T 6300
Popcom X100	Columbia
Qubie	Commodore 64
	Compaq
	Eagle
	Epson QX-10
	Hewlett-Packard HP-150
	Kaypro
	NorthStar Dimension
	Panasonic Sr. Partner
	Radio Shack RS-100

How To Read the Charts

To find the chart with the particular modem-computer combination that you wish to connect, look in the Jump Table or read the title in the upper right corner of the pages in this chapter. Each drawing's title gives the name of the modem and the name of the computer to which it is connected (see Fig. 5-1).

Moving to the center and down the page, you will find the area set aside for the cable diagram. This diagram pictures the computer with its appropriate connector on the left side of the page. The modem is pictured with its corresponding connector on the right side of the page. In the middle of the page, between the computer and the modem, you will see the connectors that you need on the cable to join the computer and the modem.

If space is cramped, which occurs with some of the diagrams, a box with the connector pin assignments is pictured below the cable connectors. This box gives the pin assignments on both ends of the cable so that when you connect the wires in the cables to the connectors, you're sure of passing the correct information. In some cases a wire in the cable does not connect to one of the pins. Typically, this wire is a type of ground, which will be connected to the shell of the cable connector itself.

At the bottom of some of the diagrams is a box that shows the positions to which the DIP switches should be set in order to ensure

Fig. 5-1. Sample modem/computer chart.

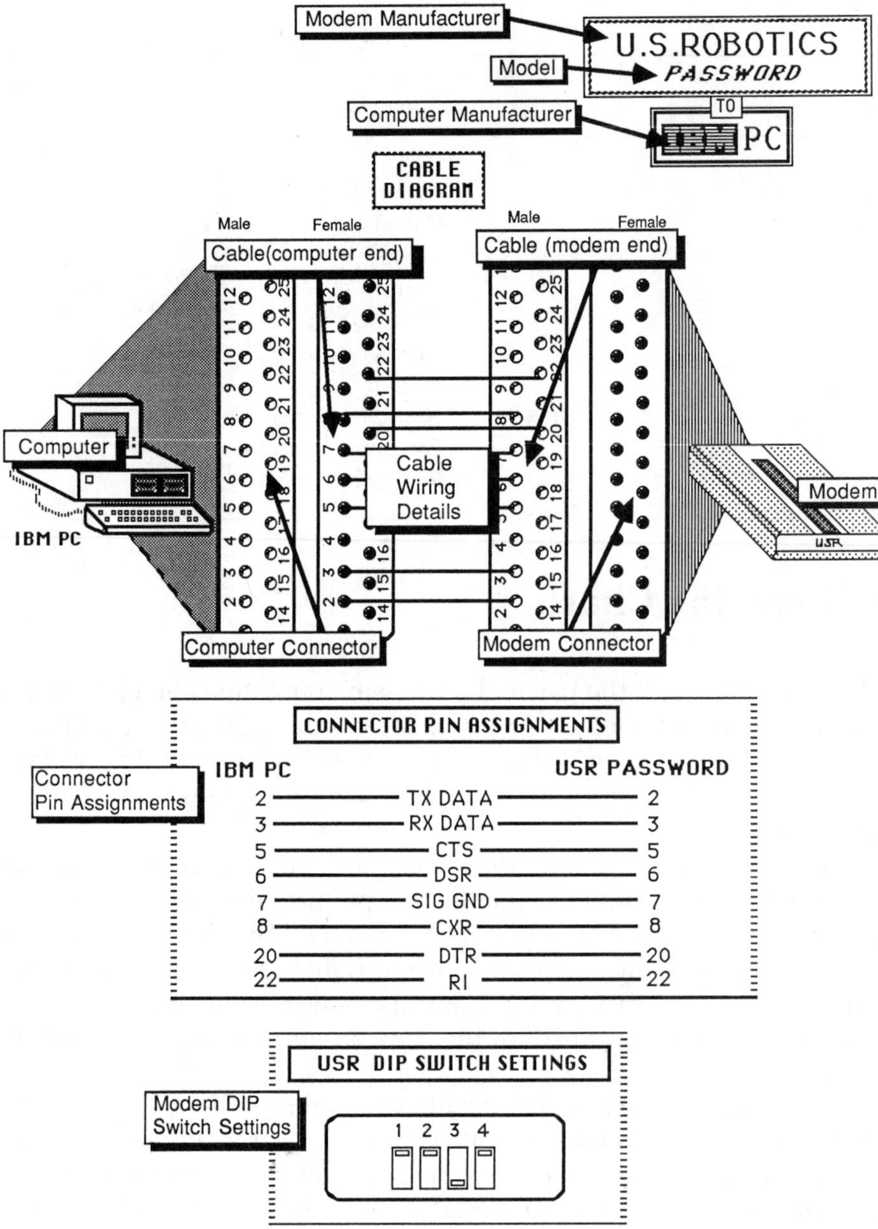

proper functioning of that modem with that computer. Pay particular attention to these switch settings.

Occasionally you will find additional text on the diagram to give further instructions in connecting your computer and modem. Before you get started, check to see whether you need to refer to your user's manual.

You might find it useful to color code your chart to correspond to the color of wires that you will be using, should you choose to make up your cables yourself. See Appendixes E and F for details and things to watch for in making your cables.

Jump Table

Jump Table—cont.

Jump Table—cont.

Jump Table—cont.

Other Computers

AT&T 6300 (For all modems, use the drawings for IBM PC.)

Columbia (For all modems, use the drawings for IBM PC.)

Commodore 64 (Buy the serial adapter, then use pinout from IBM PC drawings.)

COMPAQ (For all modems, use the drawings for IBM PC.)

Eagle (For all modems, use the drawings for IBM PC.)

EPSON QX-10 (For all modems, use the drawings for IBM PC.)

Hewlett-Packard HP-150 (For all modems, use the drawings for IBM PC.)

Kaypro (For all modems, use the drawings for IBM PC.)

Northstar Dimension (For all modems, use the drawings for IBM PC.)

Panasonic Sr. Partner (For all modems, use the drawings for IBM PC.)

Radio Shack RS-100 (For all modems, use the drawings for IBM PC.)

Other Modems

Cermetek (Use pinout from Racal-Vadic 1200V drawings and the DIP switch settings shown in Fig. 5-2.)

Fig. 5-2.   DIP switch settings for Cermetek modem.

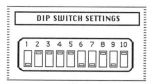

Hayes 2400 (Use same pinouts as Hayes Smartmodem drawings. Because the Hayes 2400 has no switches, disregard switch information.)

Novation 2400 (Use same pinouts as Novation Smart-Cat drawings and DIP switch settings shown in Fig. 5-3.)

Fig. 5-3.   DIP switch settings for Novation 2400 modem.

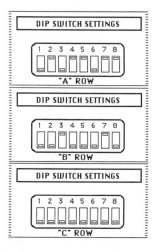

PopcomX100 (Use same pinouts as Racal-Vadic 1200V drawings.)

Qubie (Use same pinouts as Racal-Vadic 1200V drawings.)

Racal-Vadic 1200PA (Use same pinouts as Racal-Vadic 1200V. Set option 3 to 1 from the front panel. If you plan to use MNP error-correcting mode, set option 19 to 1. This will automatically recognize if a system running MNP is on the other end.

U.S. Robotics Courier 2400 (Use same pinouts as U.S. Robotics Password and DIP switch settings shown in Fig. 5-4.)

Fig. 5-4.   DIP switch settings for U.S. Robotics Courier 2400.

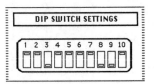

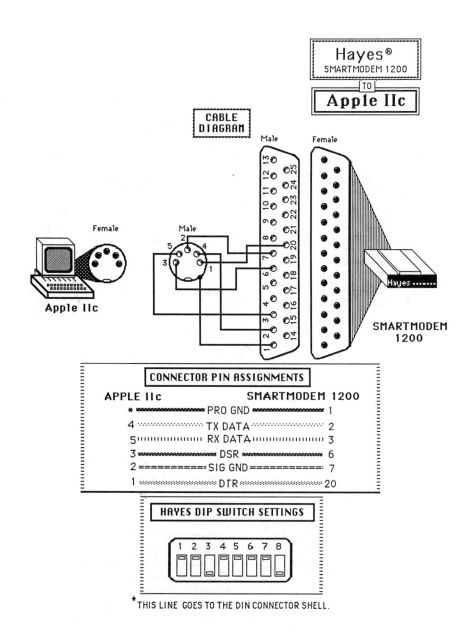

CHARTS AND DRAWINGS **63**

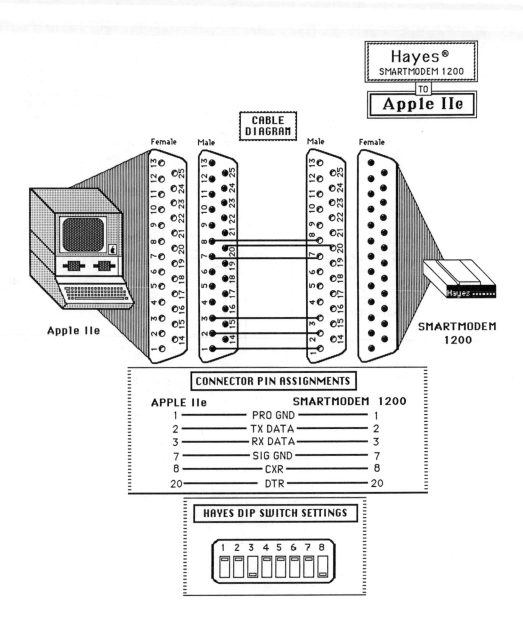

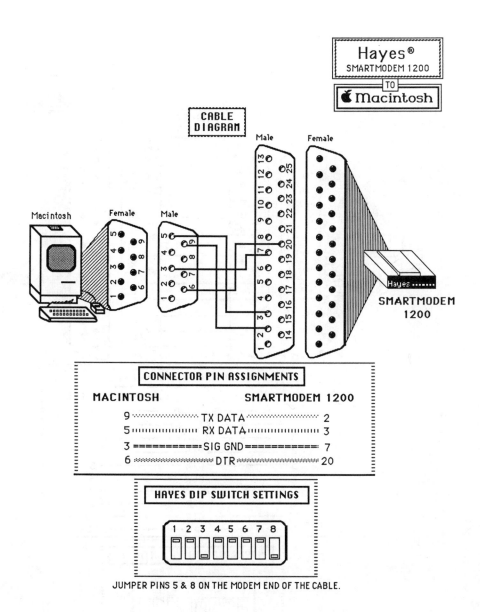

Hayes® SMARTMODEM 1200 TO Macintosh

CABLE DIAGRAM

CONNECTOR PIN ASSIGNMENTS

MACINTOSH		SMARTMODEM 1200
9	TX DATA	2
5	RX DATA	3
3	SIG GND	7
6	DTR	20

HAYES DIP SWITCH SETTINGS

1 2 3 4 5 6 7 8

JUMPER PINS 5 & 8 ON THE MODEM END OF THE CABLE.

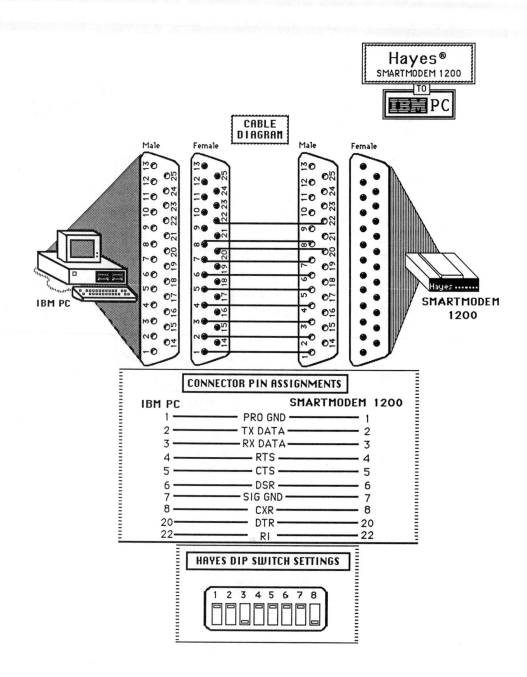

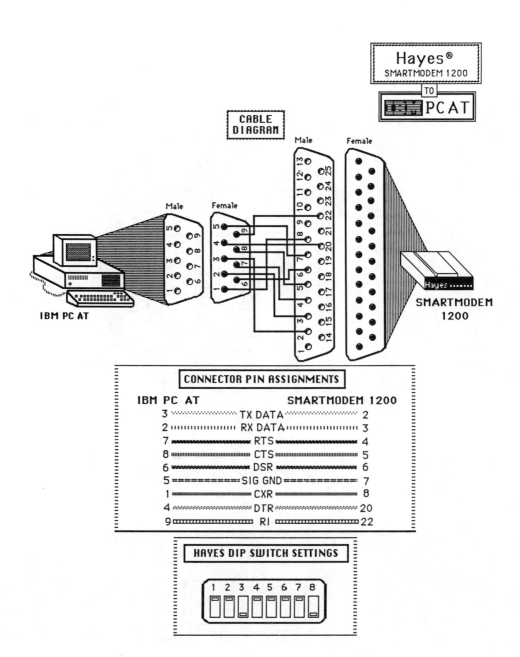

CABLE
DIAGRAM

Hayes®
SMARTMODEM 1200
TO
IBM PC AT

IBM PC AT

SMARTMODEM
1200

CONNECTOR PIN ASSIGNMENTS

IBM PC AT		SMARTMODEM 1200
3	TX DATA	2
2	RX DATA	3
7	RTS	4
8	CTS	5
6	DSR	6
5	SIG GND	7
1	CXR	8
4	DTR	20
9	RI	22

HAYES DIP SWITCH SETTINGS

1 2 3 4 5 6 7 8

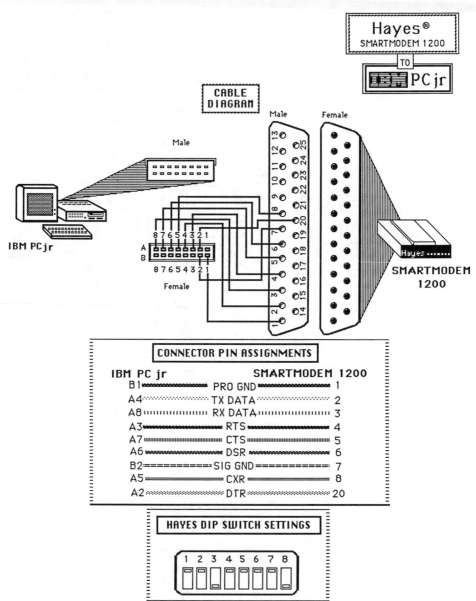

CABLE DIAGRAM

Hayes®
SMARTMODEM 1200
TO
IBM PCjr

IBM PCjr

SMARTMODEM 1200

CONNECTOR PIN ASSIGNMENTS

IBM PC jr		SMARTMODEM 1200
B1	PRO GND	1
A4	TX DATA	2
A8	RX DATA	3
A3	RTS	4
A7	CTS	5
A6	DSR	6
B2	SIG GND	7
A5	CXR	8
A2	DTR	20

HAYES DIP SWITCH SETTINGS

1 2 3 4 5 6 7 8

THE PC JR SERIAL PORT SHOULD BE SET UP AS COM 2.

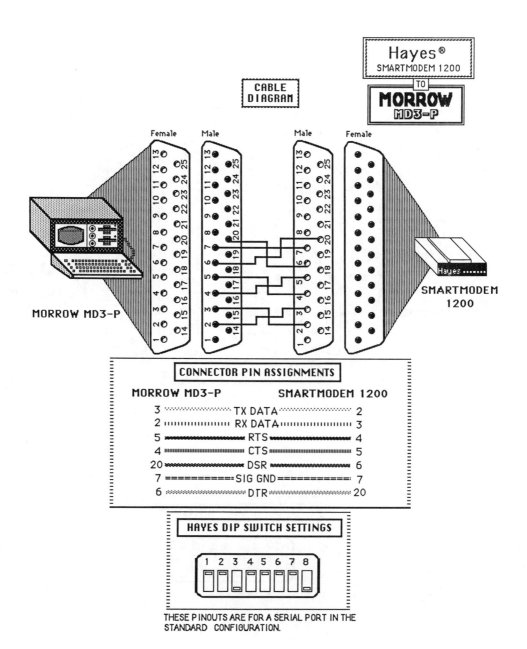

CABLE DIAGRAM

Hayes®
SMARTMODEM 1200
TO
MORROW MD3-P

Female   Male   Male   Female

MORROW MD3-P

SMARTMODEM 1200

CONNECTOR PIN ASSIGNMENTS

MORROW MD3-P		SMARTMODEM 1200
3	TX DATA	2
2	RX DATA	3
5	RTS	4
4	CTS	5
20	DSR	6
7	SIG GND	7
6	DTR	20

HAYES DIP SWITCH SETTINGS

1 2 3 4 5 6 7 8

THESE PINOUTS ARE FOR A SERIAL PORT IN THE
STANDARD CONFIGURATION.

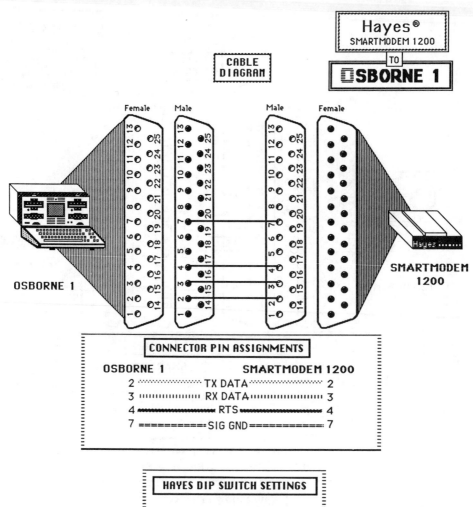

CABLE DIAGRAM

Hayes®
SMARTMODEM 1200
TO
OSBORNE 1

OSBORNE 1

SMARTMODEM 1200

CONNECTOR PIN ASSIGNMENTS

OSBORNE 1		SMARTMODEM 1200
2	TX DATA	2
3	RX DATA	3
4	RTS	4
7	SIG GND	7

HAYES DIP SWITCH SETTINGS

1 2 3 4 5 6 7 8

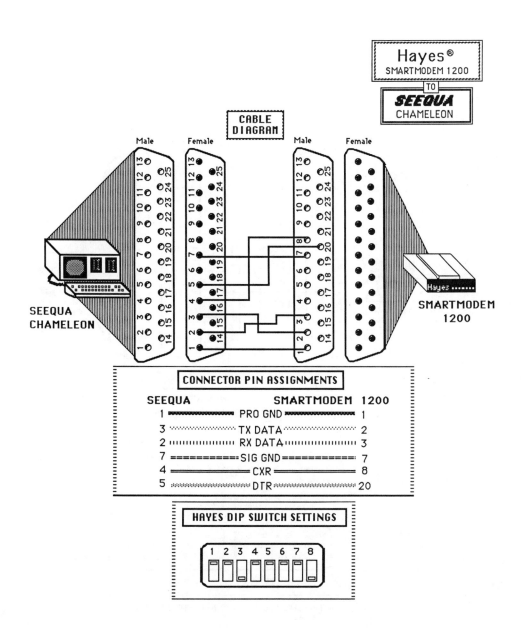

Hayes®
SMARTMODEM 1200
TO
SEEQUA
CHAMELEON

CABLE
DIAGRAM

Male   Female   Male   Female

SEEQUA
CHAMELEON

SMARTMODEM
1200

CONNECTOR PIN ASSIGNMENTS

SEEQUA		SMARTMODEM 1200
1	PRO GND	1
3	TX DATA	2
2	RX DATA	3
7	SIG GND	7
4	CXR	8
5	DTR	20

HAYES DIP SWITCH SETTINGS

1 2 3 4 5 6 7 8

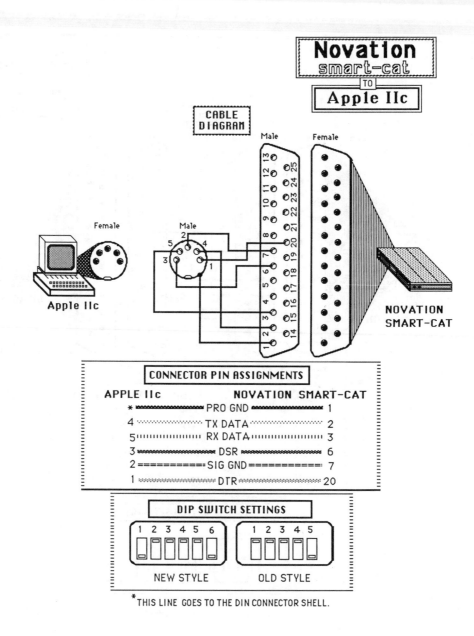

Novation smart-cat TO **Apple IIc**

CABLE DIAGRAM

Male   Female

Female   Male

Apple IIc

NOVATION SMART-CAT

CONNECTOR PIN ASSIGNMENTS

APPLE IIc		NOVATION SMART-CAT
*	PRO GND	1
4	TX DATA	2
5	RX DATA	3
3	DSR	6
2	SIG GND	7
1	DTR	20

DIP SWITCH SETTINGS

1 2 3 4 5 6

1 2 3 4 5

NEW STYLE   OLD STYLE

*THIS LINE GOES TO THE DIN CONNECTOR SHELL.

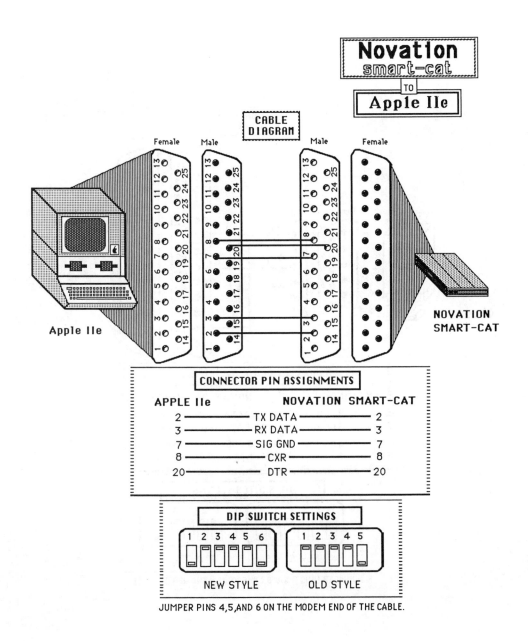

Novation smart-cat
TO
Apple IIe

CABLE DIAGRAM

Female   Male   Male   Female

Apple IIe

NOVATION
SMART-CAT

CONNECTOR PIN ASSIGNMENTS

APPLE IIe		NOVATION SMART-CAT
2	TX DATA	2
3	RX DATA	3
7	SIG GND	7
8	CXR	8
20	DTR	20

DIP SWITCH SETTINGS

1 2 3 4 5 6

1 2 3 4 5

NEW STYLE   OLD STYLE

JUMPER PINS 4,5,AND 6 ON THE MODEM END OF THE CABLE.

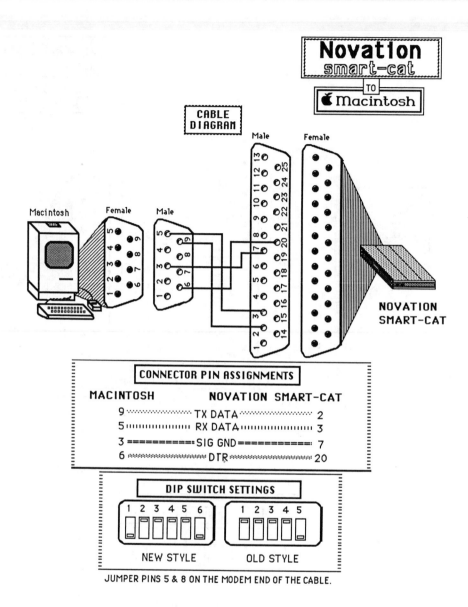

CABLE DIAGRAM

Novation smart-cat TO Macintosh

CONNECTOR PIN ASSIGNMENTS

MACINTOSH   NOVATION SMART-CAT

9 ················· TX DATA ················· 2
5 ‖‖‖‖‖‖‖‖‖‖‖‖ RX DATA ‖‖‖‖‖‖‖‖‖‖‖‖ 3
3 =========== SIG GND =========== 7
6 ▨▨▨▨▨▨▨▨▨ DTR ▨▨▨▨▨▨▨▨▨ 20

DIP SWITCH SETTINGS

NEW STYLE   OLD STYLE

JUMPER PINS 5 & 8 ON THE MODEM END OF THE CABLE.

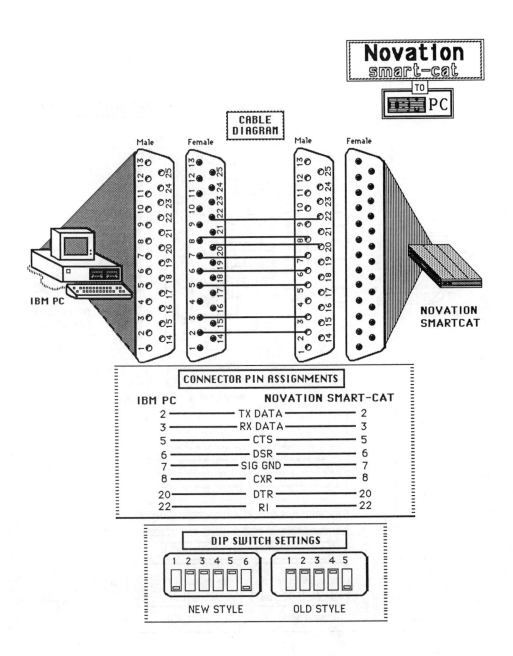

Novation smart-cat TO IBM PC

CABLE DIAGRAM

IBM PC

NOVATION SMARTCAT

CONNECTOR PIN ASSIGNMENTS

IBM PC		NOVATION SMART-CAT
2	TX DATA	2
3	RX DATA	3
5	CTS	5
6	DSR	6
7	SIG GND	7
8	CXR	8
20	DTR	20
22	RI	22

DIP SWITCH SETTINGS

1 2 3 4 5 6   1 2 3 4 5

NEW STYLE   OLD STYLE

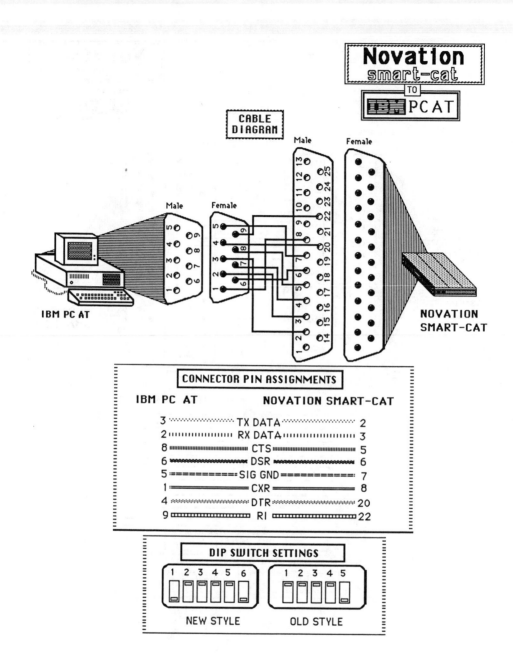

Novation smart-cat TO IBM PC AT

CABLE DIAGRAM

IBM PC AT

NOVATION SMART-CAT

CONNECTOR PIN ASSIGNMENTS

IBM PC AT		NOVATION SMART-CAT
3	TX DATA	2
2	RX DATA	3
8	CTS	5
6	DSR	6
5	SIG GND	7
1	CXR	8
4	DTR	20
9	RI	22

DIP SWITCH SETTINGS

NEW STYLE   OLD STYLE

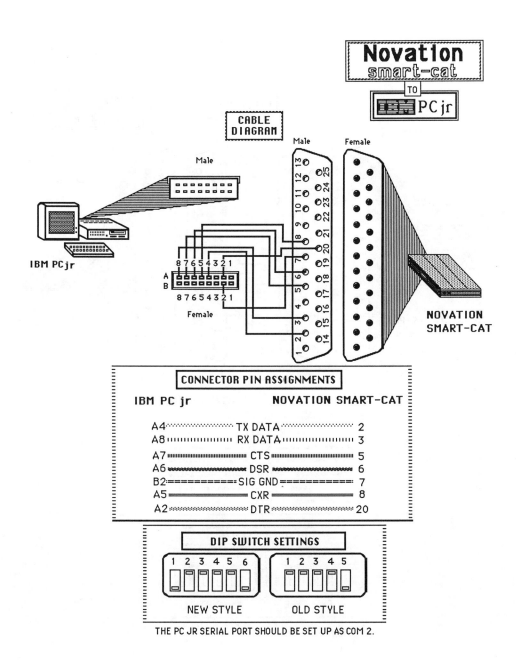

CABLE DIAGRAM

Novation smart-cat TO IBM PCjr

IBM PCjr

NOVATION SMART-CAT

CONNECTOR PIN ASSIGNMENTS

IBM PC jr		NOVATION SMART-CAT
A4	TX DATA	2
A8	RX DATA	3
A7	CTS	5
A6	DSR	6
B2	SIG GND	7
A5	CXR	8
A2	DTR	20

DIP SWITCH SETTINGS

1 2 3 4 5 6

NEW STYLE

1 2 3 4 5

OLD STYLE

THE PC JR SERIAL PORT SHOULD BE SET UP AS COM 2.

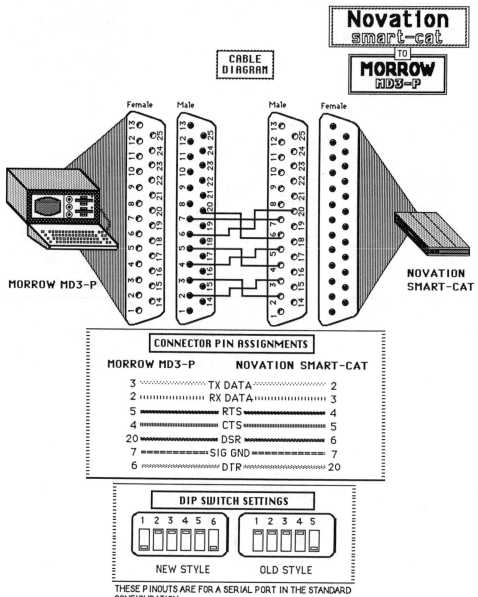

CABLE DIAGRAM

Novation smart-cat TO MORROW MD3-P

Female Male Male Female

MORROW MD3-P

NOVATION SMART-CAT

CONNECTOR PIN ASSIGNMENTS

MORROW MD3-P   NOVATION SMART-CAT

3	TX DATA	2
2	RX DATA	3
5	RTS	4
4	CTS	5
20	DSR	6
7	SIG GND	7
6	DTR	20

DIP SWITCH SETTINGS

1 2 3 4 5 6   1 2 3 4 5

NEW STYLE   OLD STYLE

THESE PINOUTS ARE FOR A SERIAL PORT IN THE STANDARD CONFIGURATION.

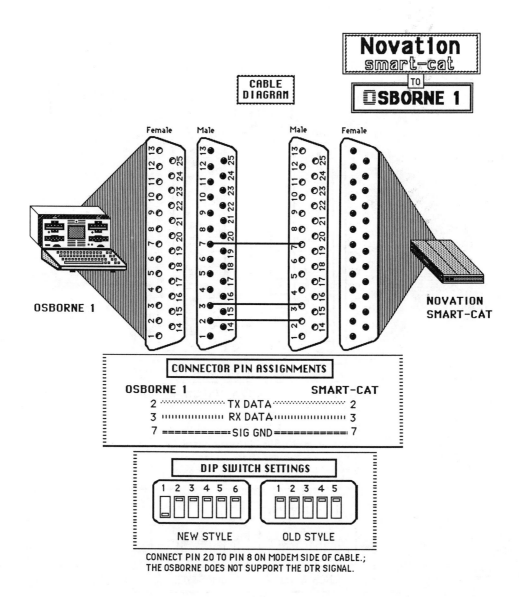

CABLE DIAGRAM

Novation smart-cat TO **OSBORNE 1**

OSBORNE 1

NOVATION SMART-CAT

CONNECTOR PIN ASSIGNMENTS

OSBORNE 1		SMART-CAT
2	TX DATA	2
3	RX DATA	3
7	SIG GND	7

DIP SWITCH SETTINGS

1 2 3 4 5 6
NEW STYLE

1 2 3 4 5
OLD STYLE

CONNECT PIN 20 TO PIN 8 ON MODEM SIDE OF CABLE.;
THE OSBORNE DOES NOT SUPPORT THE DTR SIGNAL.

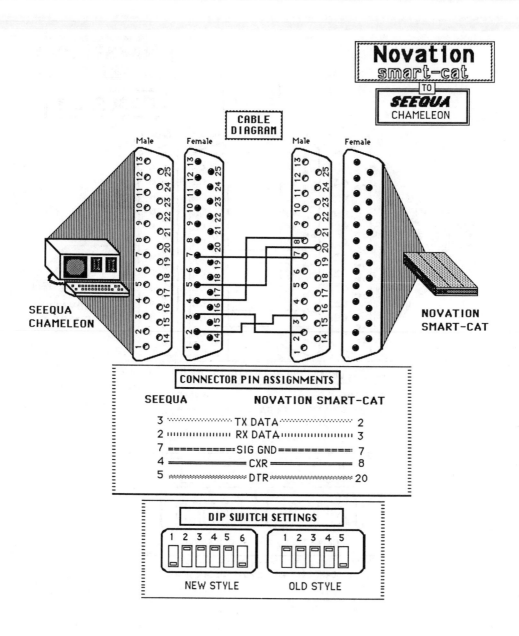

Novation smart-cat TO SEEQUA CHAMELEON

CABLE DIAGRAM

Male Female   Male Female

SEEQUA CHAMELEON

NOVATION SMART-CAT

CONNECTOR PIN ASSIGNMENTS

SEEQUA		NOVATION SMART-CAT
3	TX DATA	2
2	RX DATA	3
7	SIG GND	7
4	CXR	8
5	DTR	20

DIP SWITCH SETTINGS

1 2 3 4 5 6

NEW STYLE

1 2 3 4 5

OLD STYLE

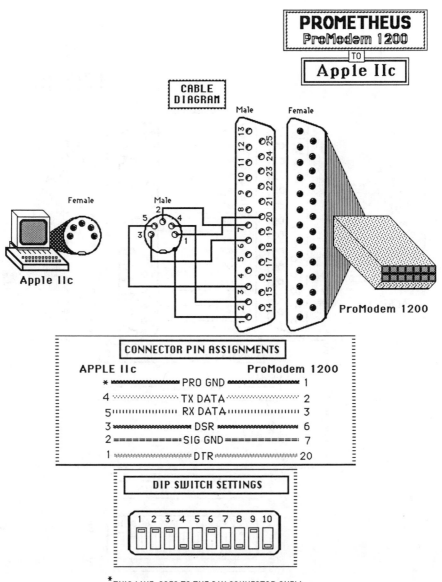

PROMETHEUS
ProModem 1200
TO
Apple IIc

CABLE DIAGRAM

Apple IIc

ProModem 1200

CONNECTOR PIN ASSIGNMENTS

APPLE IIc		ProModem 1200
*	PRO GND	1
4	TX DATA	2
5	RX DATA	3
3	DSR	6
2	SIG GND	7
1	DTR	20

DIP SWITCH SETTINGS

1 2 3 4 5 6 7 8 9 10

*THIS LINE GOES TO THE DIN CONNECTOR SHELL.

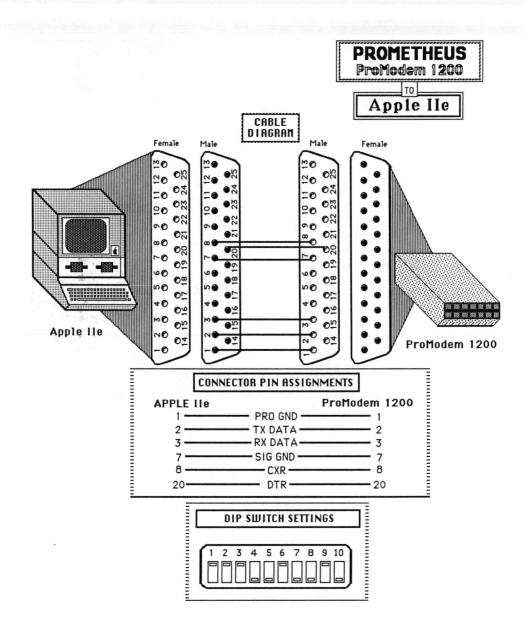

PROMETHEUS
ProModem 1200
TO
Apple IIe

CABLE DIAGRAM

Female   Male   Male   Female

Apple IIe

ProModem 1200

CONNECTOR PIN ASSIGNMENTS

APPLE IIe		ProModem 1200
1	PRO GND	1
2	TX DATA	2
3	RX DATA	3
7	SIG GND	7
8	CXR	8
20	DTR	20

DIP SWITCH SETTINGS

1 2 3 4 5 6 7 8 9 10

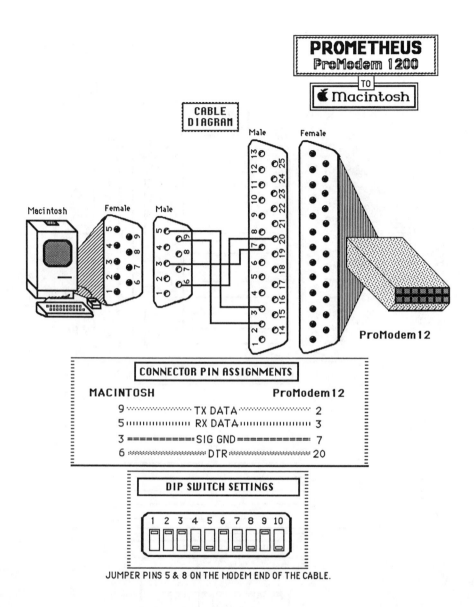

PROMETHEUS
ProModem 1200
TO
🍎 Macintosh

CABLE
DIAGRAM

CONNECTOR PIN ASSIGNMENTS

MACINTOSH		ProModem12
9	~~~~~~~ TX DATA ~~~~~~~	2
5	IIIIIIIIIIIII RX DATA IIIIIIIIIIIII	3
3	========== SIG GND ==========	7
6	~~~~~~~~~~ DTR ~~~~~~~~~~	20

DIP SWITCH SETTINGS

1 2 3 4 5 6 7 8 9 10

JUMPER PINS 5 & 8 ON THE MODEM END OF THE CABLE.

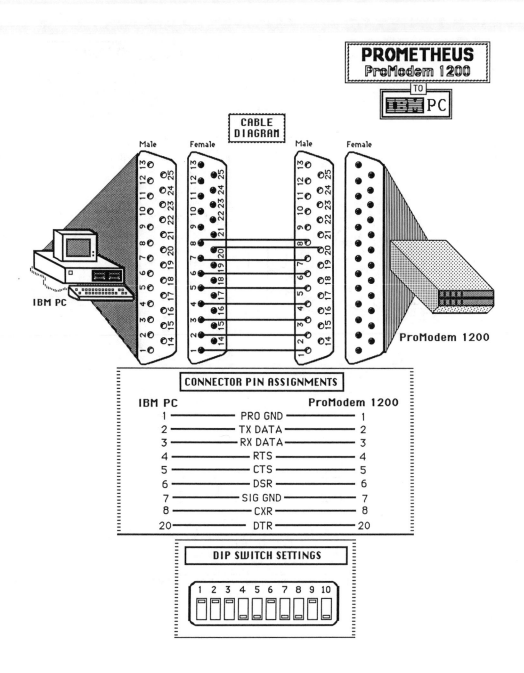

PROMETHEUS
ProModem 1200

TO

IBM PC

CABLE DIAGRAM

Male   Female   Male   Female

IBM PC

ProModem 1200

CONNECTOR PIN ASSIGNMENTS

IBM PC		ProModem 1200
1	PRO GND	1
2	TX DATA	2
3	RX DATA	3
4	RTS	4
5	CTS	5
6	DSR	6
7	SIG GND	7
8	CXR	8
20	DTR	20

DIP SWITCH SETTINGS

1 2 3 4 5 6 7 8 9 10

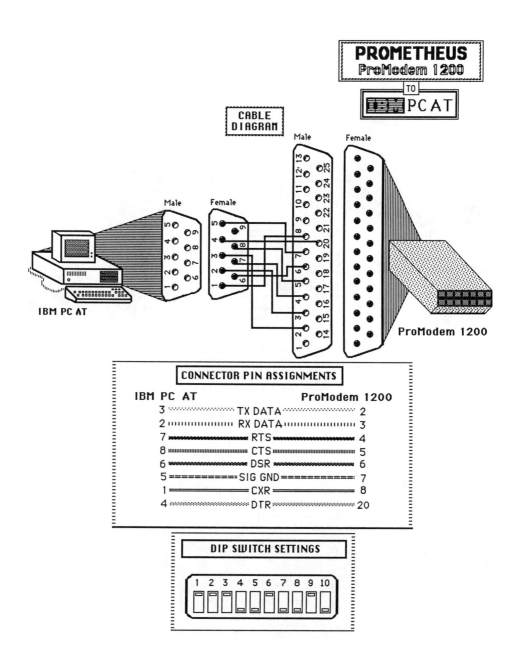

PROMETHEUS
ProModem 1200
TO
IBM PC AT

CABLE DIAGRAM

IBM PC AT

ProModem 1200

CONNECTOR PIN ASSIGNMENTS

IBM PC AT		ProModem 1200
3	TX DATA	2
2	RX DATA	3
7	RTS	4
8	CTS	5
6	DSR	6
5	SIG GND	7
1	CXR	8
4	DTR	20

DIP SWITCH SETTINGS

1 2 3 4 5 6 7 8 9 10

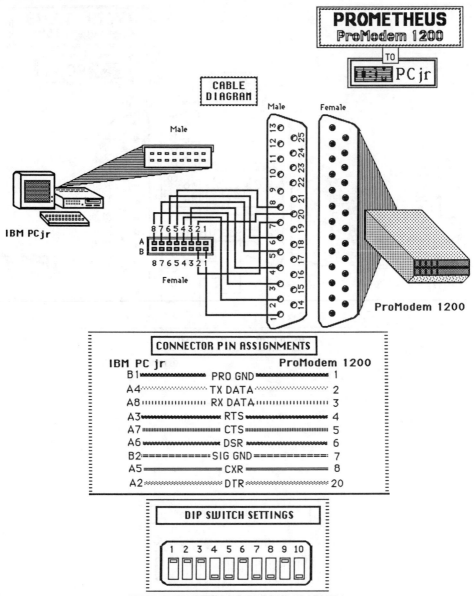

PROMETHEUS
PreModem 1200
TO
IBM PC jr

CABLE DIAGRAM

IBM PCjr

ProModem 1200

CONNECTOR PIN ASSIGNMENTS

IBM PC jr		ProModem 1200
B1	PRO GND	1
A4	TX DATA	2
A8	RX DATA	3
A3	RTS	4
A7	CTS	5
A6	DSR	6
B2	SIG GND	7
A5	CXR	8
A2	DTR	20

DIP SWITCH SETTINGS

1 2 3 4 5 6 7 8 9 10

THE PC JR SERIAL PORT SHOULD BE SET UP AS COM 2.

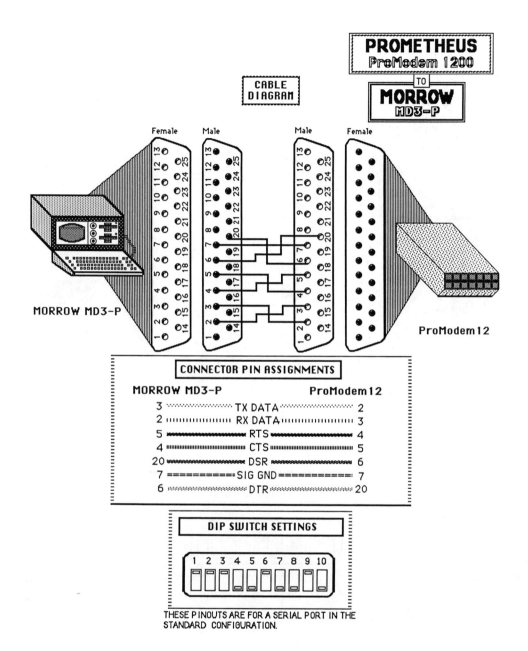

CABLE DIAGRAM

PROMETHEUS ProModem 1200 TO MORROW MD3-P

MORROW MD3-P

ProModem12

CONNECTOR PIN ASSIGNMENTS

MORROW MD3-P		ProModem12
3	TX DATA	2
2	RX DATA	3
5	RTS	4
4	CTS	5
20	DSR	6
7	SIG GND	7
6	DTR	20

DIP SWITCH SETTINGS

1 2 3 4 5 6 7 8 9 10

THESE PINOUTS ARE FOR A SERIAL PORT IN THE
STANDARD CONFIGURATION.

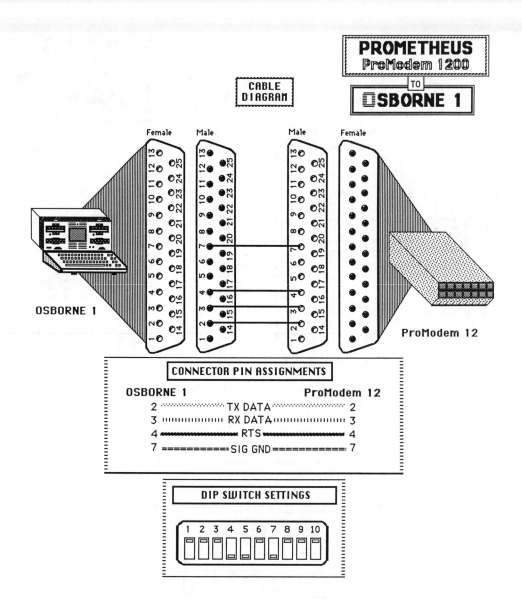

CABLE DIAGRAM

PROMETHEUS ProModem 1200 TO OSBORNE 1

Female   Male   Male   Female

OSBORNE 1

ProModem 12

CONNECTOR PIN ASSIGNMENTS

OSBORNE 1   ProModem 12

2 ~~~~~~~~~ TX DATA ~~~~~~~~~ 2
3 ''''''''''''' RX DATA ''''''''''''' 3
4 ▬▬▬▬▬▬ RTS ▬▬▬▬▬▬ 4
7 ========= SIG GND ========= 7

DIP SWITCH SETTINGS

1 2 3 4 5 6 7 8 9 10

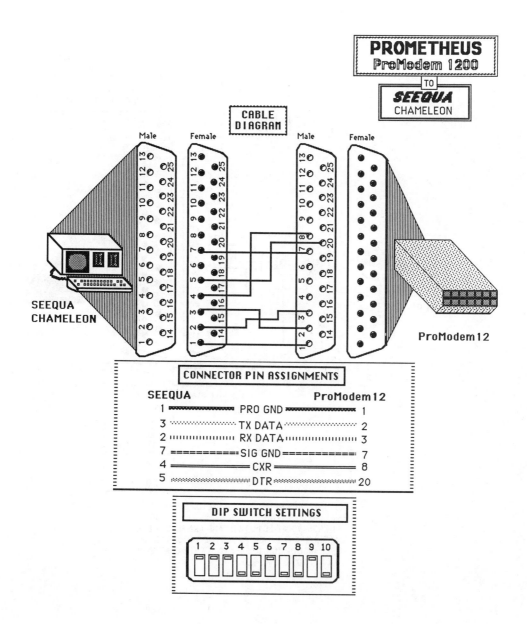

CABLE DIAGRAM

PROMETHEUS ProModem 1200 TO **SEEQUA CHAMELEON**

CONNECTOR PIN ASSIGNMENTS

SEEQUA		ProModem 12
1	PRO GND	1
3	TX DATA	2
2	RX DATA	3
7	SIG GND	7
4	CXR	8
5	DTR	20

DIP SWITCH SETTINGS

1 2 3 4 5 6 7 8 9 10

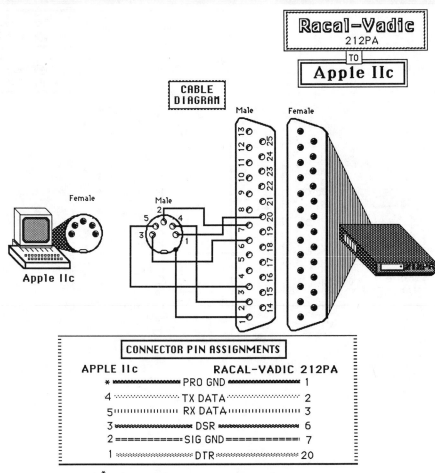

Racal-Vadic
212PA

TO

Apple IIc

CABLE DIAGRAM

CONNECTOR PIN ASSIGNMENTS

APPLE IIc		RACAL-VADIC 212PA
*	PRO GND	1
4	TX DATA	2
5	RX DATA	3
3	DSR	6
2	SIG GND	7
1	DTR	20

*THIS LINE GOES TO THE DIN CONNECTOR SHELL.
THERE ARE NO SWITCHES ON THIS MODEM. THE OPTIONS
ARE IN NON-VOLATILE MEMORY AND ARE ACCESSIBLE
FROM THE FRONT PANEL. TO SET THE OPTIONS FOR PC
USE, CHANGE OPTION 1 TO 2 AND SET THE CARRIER OP-
TION (16) TO NORMAL (2).

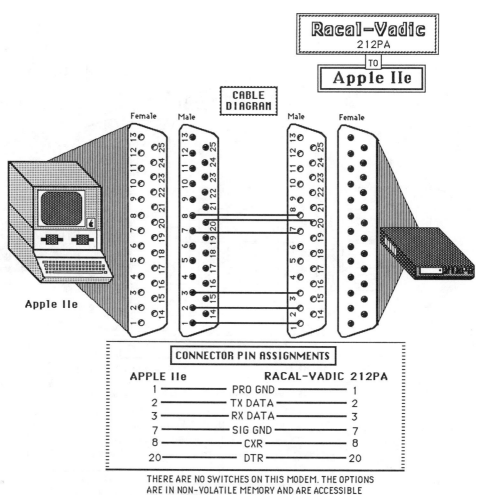

Racal-Vadic
212PA
TO
Apple IIe

CABLE DIAGRAM

Female   Male   Male   Female

Apple IIe

CONNECTOR PIN ASSIGNMENTS

APPLE IIe		RACAL-VADIC 212PA
1	PRO GND	1
2	TX DATA	2
3	RX DATA	3
7	SIG GND	7
8	CXR	8
20	DTR	20

THERE ARE NO SWITCHES ON THIS MODEM. THE OPTIONS
ARE IN NON-VOLATILE MEMORY AND ARE ACCESSIBLE
FROM THE FRONT PANEL. TO SET THE OPTIONS FOR PC
USE, CHANGE OPTION 1 TO 2 AND SET THE CARRIER OP-
TION (16) TO NORMAL (2).

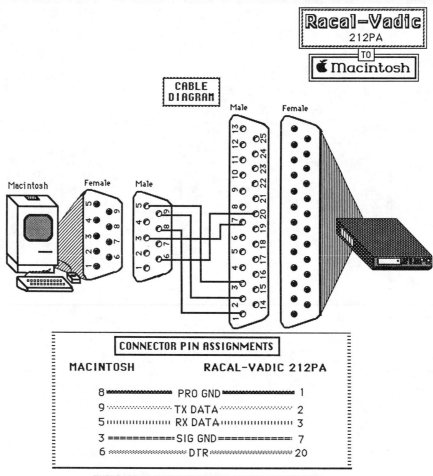

CABLE DIAGRAM

Racal-Vadic 212PA TO Macintosh

CONNECTOR PIN ASSIGNMENTS

MACINTOSH		RACAL-VADIC 212PA
8	PRO GND	1
9	TX DATA	2
5	RX DATA	3
3	SIG GND	7
6	DTR	20

THERE ARE NO SWITCHES ON THIS MODEM. THE OPTIONS
ARE IN NON-VOLATILE MEMORY AND ARE ACCESSIBLE
FROM THE FRONT PANEL. TO SET THE OPTIONS FOR PC
USE, CHANGE OPTION 1 TO 2 AND SET THE CARRIER OP-
TION (16) TO NORMAL (2).

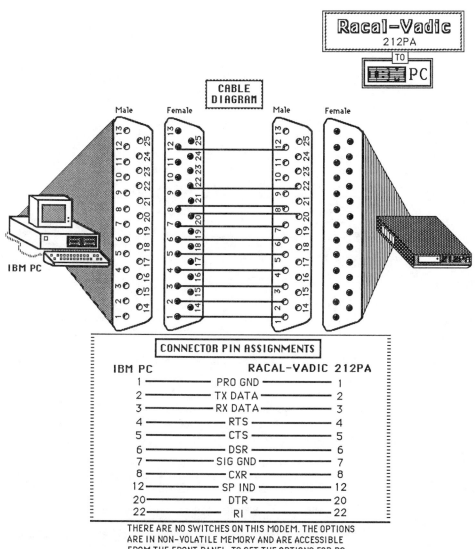

Racal-Vadic 212PA
TO
IBM PC

CABLE DIAGRAM

Male   Female   Male   Female

IBM PC

CONNECTOR PIN ASSIGNMENTS

IBM PC		RACAL-VADIC 212PA
1	PRO GND	1
2	TX DATA	2
3	RX DATA	3
4	RTS	4
5	CTS	5
6	DSR	6
7	SIG GND	7
8	CXR	8
12	SP IND	12
20	DTR	20
22	RI	22

THERE ARE NO SWITCHES ON THIS MODEM. THE OPTIONS
ARE IN NON-VOLATILE MEMORY AND ARE ACCESSIBLE
FROM THE FRONT PANEL. TO SET THE OPTIONS FOR PC
USE, CHANGE OPTION 1 TO 2 AND SET THE CARRIER OP-
TION TO NORMAL.

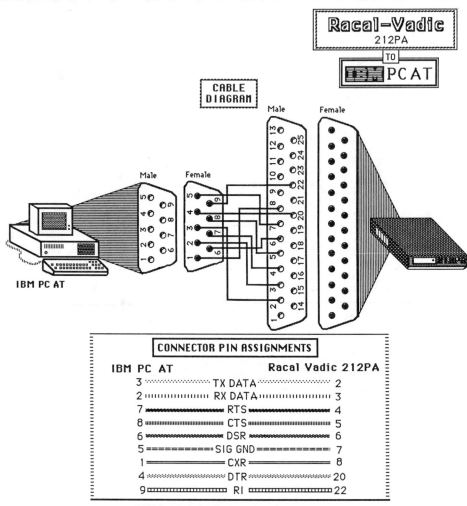

Racal-Vadic
212PA

TO

IBM PC AT

CABLE DIAGRAM

Male   Female

Male   Female

IBM PC AT

IBM PC AT		Racal Vadic 212PA
3	TX DATA	2
2	RX DATA	3
7	RTS	4
8	CTS	5
6	DSR	6
5	SIG GND	7
1	CXR	8
4	DTR	20
9	RI	22

CONNECTOR PIN ASSIGNMENTS

THERE ARE NO SWITCHES ON THIS MODEM. THE OPTIONS
ARE IN NON-VOLATILE MEMORY AND ARE ACCESSIBLE
FROM THE FRONT PANEL. TO SET THE OPTIONS FOR PC
USE, CHANGE OPTION 1 TO 2 AND SET THE CARRIER OP-
TION (16) TO NORMAL (2).

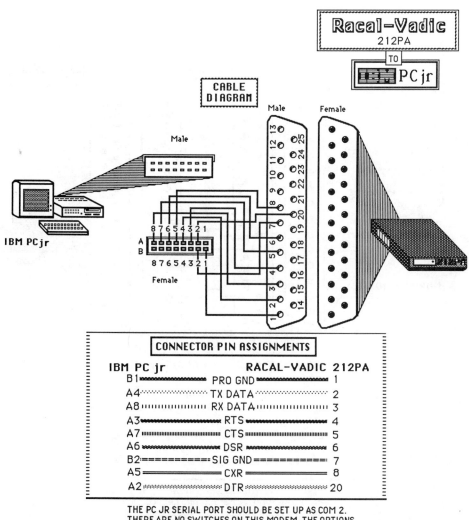

Racal-Vadic
212PA
TO
IBM PC jr

CABLE DIAGRAM

Male

IBM PCjr

Male

Female

CONNECTOR PIN ASSIGNMENTS

IBM PC jr		RACAL-VADIC 212PA
B1	PRO GND	1
A4	TX DATA	2
A8	RX DATA	3
A3	RTS	4
A7	CTS	5
A6	DSR	6
B2	SIG GND	7
A5	CXR	8
A2	DTR	20

THE PC JR SERIAL PORT SHOULD BE SET UP AS COM 2.
THERE ARE NO SWITCHES ON THIS MODEM. THE OPTIONS
ARE IN NON-VOLATILE MEMORY AND ARE ACCESSIBLE
FROM THE FRONT PANEL. TO SET THE OPTIONS FOR PC
USE, CHANGE OPTION 1 TO 2 AND SET THE CARRIER OP-
TION (16) TO NORMAL (2).

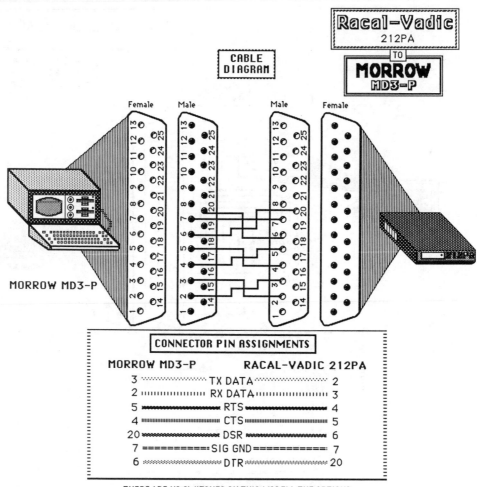

CABLE DIAGRAM

Racal-Vadic 212PA TO **MORROW** MD3-P

Female · Male · Male · Female

MORROW MD3-P

CONNECTOR PIN ASSIGNMENTS

MORROW MD3-P		RACAL-VADIC 212PA
3	TX DATA	2
2	RX DATA	3
5	RTS	4
4	CTS	5
20	DSR	6
7	SIG GND	7
6	DTR	20

THERE ARE NO SWITCHES ON THIS MODEM. THE OPTIONS ARE IN NON-VOLATILE MEMORY AND ARE ACCESSIBLE FROM THE FRONT PANEL. TO SET THE OPTIONS FOR PC USE, CHANGE OPTION 1 TO 2 AND SET THE CARRIER OPTION (16) TO NORMAL (2). THESE PINOUTS ARE FOR A SERIAL PORT IN THE STANDARD CONFIGURATION.

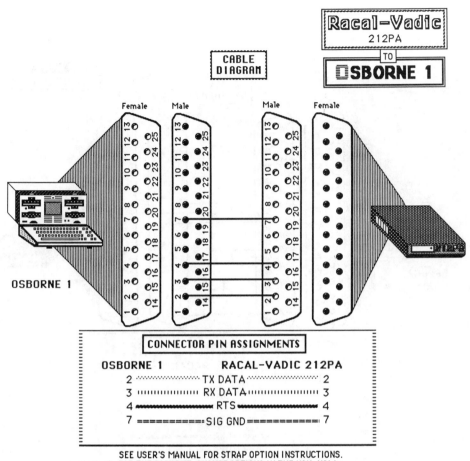

CABLE DIAGRAM

Racal-Vadic
212PA

TO

⬛SBORNE 1

Female   Male   Male   Female

OSBORNE 1

CONNECTOR PIN ASSIGNMENTS

OSBORNE 1		RACAL-VADIC 212PA
2	TX DATA	2
3	RX DATA	3
4	RTS	4
7	SIG GND	7

SEE USER'S MANUAL FOR STRAP OPTION INSTRUCTIONS.
FOR THE OSBORNE, CHANGE OPTIONS IN THE NON-VOLA-
TILE MEMORY: OPTION 1 CHANGES TO 2, THEN SET CXR
AND DTR TO "FORCED ON".

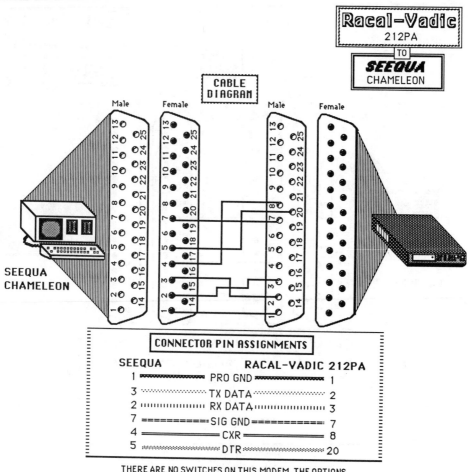

CABLE DIAGRAM

Racal-Vadic 212PA
TO
SEEQUA CHAMELEON

CONNECTOR PIN ASSIGNMENTS

SEEQUA		RACAL-VADIC 212PA
1	PRO GND	1
3	TX DATA	2
2	RX DATA	3
7	SIG GND	7
4	CXR	8
5	DTR	20

THERE ARE NO SWITCHES ON THIS MODEM. THE OPTIONS
ARE IN NON-VOLATILE MEMORY AND ARE ACCESSIBLE
FROM THE FRONT PANEL. TO SET THE OPTIONS FOR PC
USE, CHANGE OPTION 1 TO 2 AND SET THE CARRIER OP-
TION (16) TO NORMAL (2).

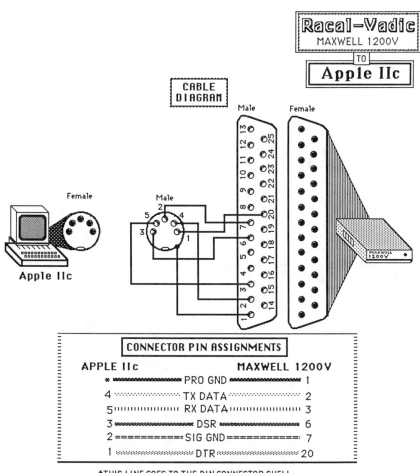

Racal-Vadic
MAXWELL 1200V
TO
Apple IIc

CABLE DIAGRAM

Male   Female

Female

Male

Apple IIc

CONNECTOR PIN ASSIGNMENTS

APPLE IIc		MAXWELL 1200V
*	PRO GND	1
4	TX DATA	2
5	RX DATA	3
3	DSR	6
2	SIG GND	7
1	DTR	20

*THIS LINE GOES TO THE DIN CONNECTOR SHELL.
THERE ARE NO SWITCHES ON THIS MODEM. IT IS
PRE-CONFIGURED FOR PC USERS. REFER TO USER'S
MANUAL FOR DISCUSSION OF OPTIONAL SETTINGS.
THIS MODEM WILL AUTODIAL USING RACAL-VADIC
OR HAYES COMMAND SETS.

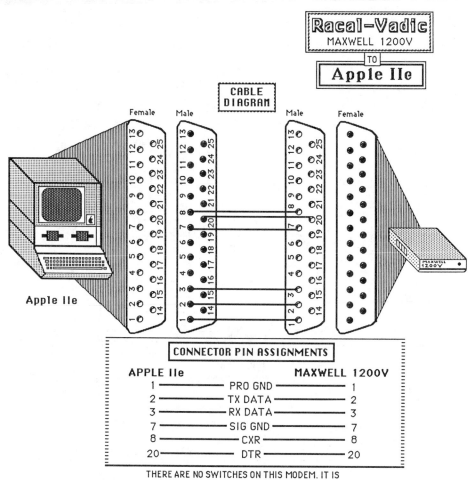

Racal-Vadic
MAXWELL 1200V
TO
Apple IIe

CABLE
DIAGRAM

Female   Male   Male   Female

Apple IIe

CONNECTOR PIN ASSIGNMENTS

APPLE IIe   MAXWELL 1200V
1 ——————— PRO GND ——————— 1
2 ——————— TX DATA ——————— 2
3 ——————— RX DATA ——————— 3
7 ——————— SIG GND ——————— 7
8 ——————————— CXR ——————————— 8
20 ——————— DTR ——————— 20

THERE ARE NO SWITCHES ON THIS MODEM. IT IS
PRE-CONFIGURED FOR PC USERS. REFER TO USER'S
MANUAL FOR DISCUSSION OF OPTIONAL SETTINGS.
THIS MODEM WILL AUTODIAL USING RACAL-VADIC OR
HAYES COMMAND SETS.

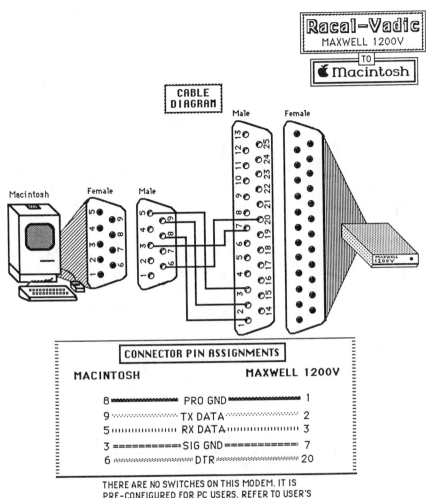

Racal-Vadic
MAXWELL 1200V
TO
🍎 Macintosh

CABLE DIAGRAM

CONNECTOR PIN ASSIGNMENTS

MACINTOSH		MAXWELL 1200V
8	PRO GND	1
9	TX DATA	2
5	RX DATA	3
3	SIG GND	7
6	DTR	20

THERE ARE NO SWITCHES ON THIS MODEM. IT IS
PRE-CONFIGURED FOR PC USERS. REFER TO USER'S
MANUAL FOR DISCUSSION OF OPTIONAL SETTINGS.
THIS MODEM WILL AUTODIAL USING RACAL-VADIC OR
HAYES COMMAND SETS. JUMPER PINS 5 & 8 ON THE
MODEM END OF THE CABLE.

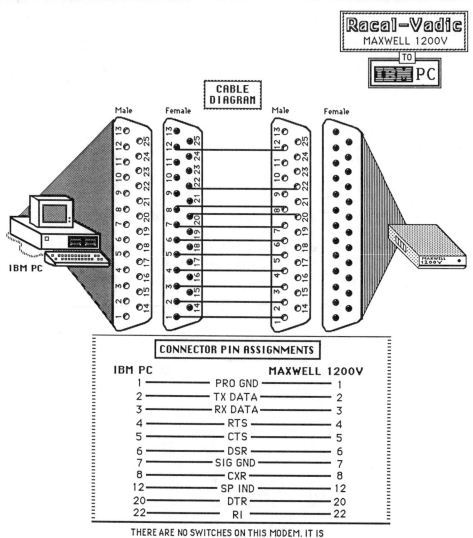

Racal-Vadic
MAXWELL 1200V
TO
IBM PC

CABLE DIAGRAM

Male   Female   Male   Female

CONNECTOR PIN ASSIGNMENTS

IBM PC		MAXWELL 1200V
1	PRO GND	1
2	TX DATA	2
3	RX DATA	3
4	RTS	4
5	CTS	5
6	DSR	6
7	SIG GND	7
8	CXR	8
12	SP IND	12
20	DTR	20
22	RI	22

THERE ARE NO SWITCHES ON THIS MODEM. IT IS
PRE-CONFIGURED FOR PC USERS. REFER TO USER'S
MANUAL FOR DISCUSSION OF OPTIONAL SETTINGS.
THIS MODEM WILL AUTODIAL USING RACAL-VADIC OR
HAYES COMMAND SETS.

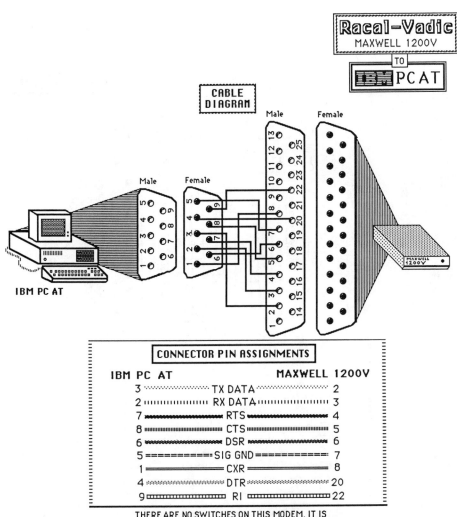

Racal-Vadic
MAXWELL 1200V
TO
IBM PC AT

CABLE DIAGRAM

IBM PC AT

CONNECTOR PIN ASSIGNMENTS

IBM PC AT		MAXWELL 1200V
3	TX DATA	2
2	RX DATA	3
7	RTS	4
8	CTS	5
6	DSR	6
5	SIG GND	7
1	CXR	8
4	DTR	20
9	RI	22

THERE ARE NO SWITCHES ON THIS MODEM. IT IS
PRE-CONFIGURED FOR PC USERS. REFER TO USER'S
MANUAL FOR DISCUSSION OF OPTIONAL SETTINGS.
THIS MODEM WILL AUTODIAL USING RACAL-VADIC OR
HAYES COMMAND SETS.

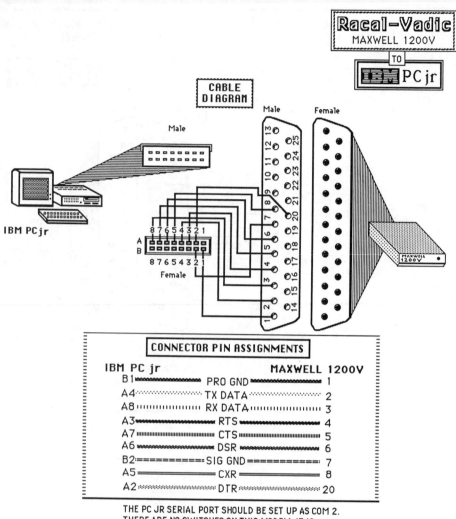

CABLE DIAGRAM

Racal-Vadic MAXWELL 1200V TO **IBM PC jr**

IBM PCjr

Male

Male

Female

A
B

8 7 6 5 4 3 2 1

8 7 6 5 4 3 2 1

Female

CONNECTOR PIN ASSIGNMENTS

IBM PC jr		MAXWELL 1200V
B1	PRO GND	1
A4	TX DATA	2
A8	RX DATA	3
A3	RTS	4
A7	CTS	5
A6	DSR	6
B2	SIG GND	7
A5	CXR	8
A2	DTR	20

THE PC JR SERIAL PORT SHOULD BE SET UP AS COM 2.
THERE ARE NO SWITCHES ON THIS MODEM. IT IS
PRE-CONFIGURED FOR PC USERS. REFER TO USER'S
MANUAL FOR DISCUSSION OF OPTIONAL SETTINGS.
THIS MODEM WILL AUTODIAL USING RACAL-VADIC OR
HAYES COMMAND SETS.

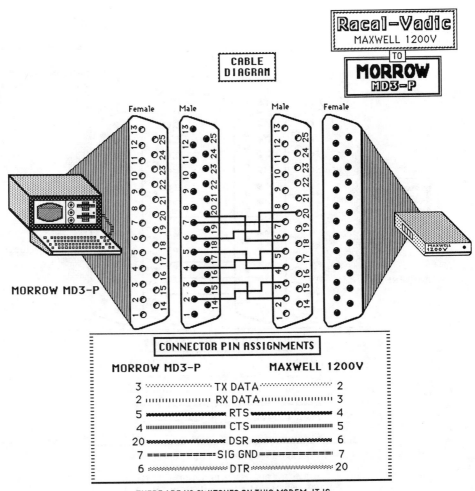

CABLE DIAGRAM

Racal-Vadic MAXWELL 1200V TO **MORROW MD3-P**

MORROW MD3-P

CONNECTOR PIN ASSIGNMENTS

MORROW MD3-P   MAXWELL 1200V

3	TX DATA	2
2	RX DATA	3
5	RTS	4
4	CTS	5
20	DSR	6
7	SIG GND	7
6	DTR	20

THERE ARE NO SWITCHES ON THIS MODEM. IT IS
PRE-CONFIGURED FOR PC USERS. REFER TO USER'S
MANUAL FOR DISCUSSION OF OPTIONAL SETTINGS.
THIS MODEM WILL AUTODIAL USING RACAL-VADIC
OR HAYES COMMAND SETS. THESE PINOUTS ARE FOR
A SERIAL PORT IN THE STANDARD CONFIGURATION.

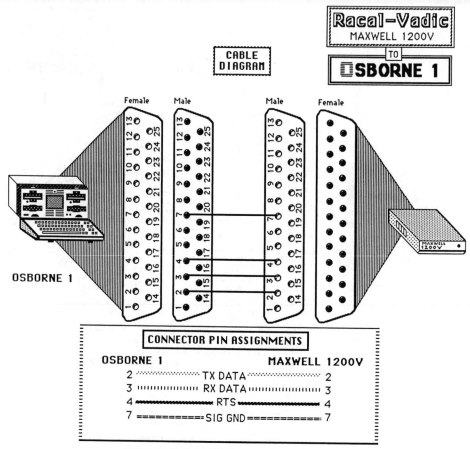

CABLE DIAGRAM

Racal-Vadic
MAXWELL 1200V
TO
SBORNE 1

Female   Male   Male   Female

OSBORNE 1

CONNECTOR PIN ASSIGNMENTS

OSBORNE 1   MAXWELL 1200V

2 ·················· TX DATA ·················· 2
3 ···················· RX DATA ···················· 3
4 ━━━━━━━━━ RTS ━━━━━━━━━ 4
7 ========== SIG GND ========== 7

THERE ARE NO SWITCHES ON THIS MODEM. IT IS
PRE-CONFIGURED FOR PC USERS. REFER TO USER'S
MANUAL FOR DISCUSSION OF OPTIONAL SETTINGS.
THIS MODEM WILL AUTODIAL USING RACAL-VADIC OR
HAYES COMMAND SETS. THE OSBORNE DOESN'T RAISE
DTR HIGH SO THIS SIGNAL MUST BE FORCED AT THE
MODEM END. SEE USER'S MANUAL FOR DETAILS.

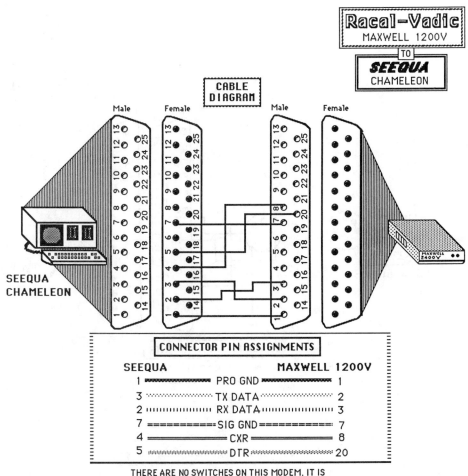

Racal-Vadic
MAXWELL 1200V
TO
SEEQUA CHAMELEON

CABLE DIAGRAM

Male Female Male Female

SEEQUA CHAMELEON

MAXWELL 1200V

CONNECTOR PIN ASSIGNMENTS

SEEQUA		MAXWELL 1200V
1	PRO GND	1
3	TX DATA	2
2	RX DATA	3
7	SIG GND	7
4	CXR	8
5	DTR	20

THERE ARE NO SWITCHES ON THIS MODEM. IT IS
PRE-CONFIGURED FOR PC USERS. REFER TO USER'S
MANUAL FOR DISCUSSION OF OPTIONAL SETTINGS.
THIS MODEM WILL AUTODIAL USING RACAL-VADIC OR
HAYES COMMAND SETS.

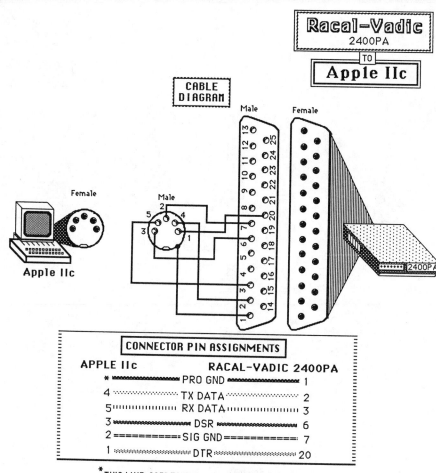

Racal-Vadic
2400PA
TO
Apple IIc

CABLE DIAGRAM

CONNECTOR PIN ASSIGNMENTS

APPLE IIc		RACAL-VADIC 2400PA
*	PRO GND	1
4	TX DATA	2
5	RX DATA	3
3	DSR	6
2	SIG GND	7
1	DTR	20

*THIS LINE GOES TO THE DIN CONNECTOR SHELL.
THERE ARE NO SWITCHES ON THIS MODEM. REFER TO
USER'S MANUAL FOR DISCUSSION OF OPTIONAL SETTINGS
IN NON-VOLATILE MEMORY. THE MODEM WILL WORK WITH
MANY SOFTWARE PACKAGES IN THE STANDARD CONFIGURA-
TION. FOR SOME PACKAGES OPTION 3 SHOULD BE SET TO 1.

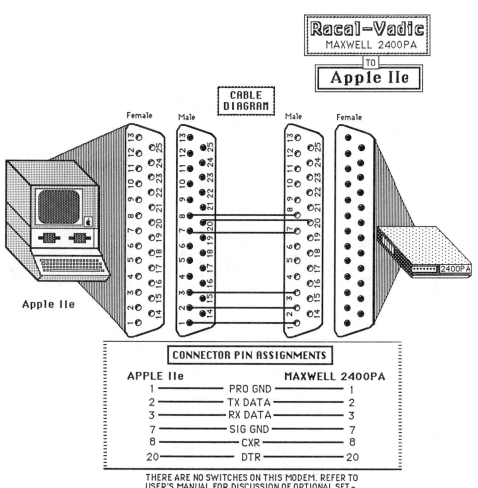

Racal–Vadic
MAXWELL 2400PA
TO
Apple IIe

CABLE DIAGRAM

Female   Male   Male   Female

Apple IIe

2400P A

CONNECTOR PIN ASSIGNMENTS

APPLE IIe		MAXWELL 2400PA
1	PRO GND	1
2	TX DATA	2
3	RX DATA	3
7	SIG GND	7
8	CXR	8
20	DTR	20

THERE ARE NO SWITCHES ON THIS MODEM. REFER TO
USER'S MANUAL FOR DISCUSSION OF OPTIONAL SET-
TINGS IN NON-VOLATILE MEMORY. THIS MODEM WILL
WORK MANY SOFTWARE PACKAGES IN THE STANDARD
CONFIGURATION. FOR SOME PACKAGES OPTION 3 SHOULD
BE SET TO 1.

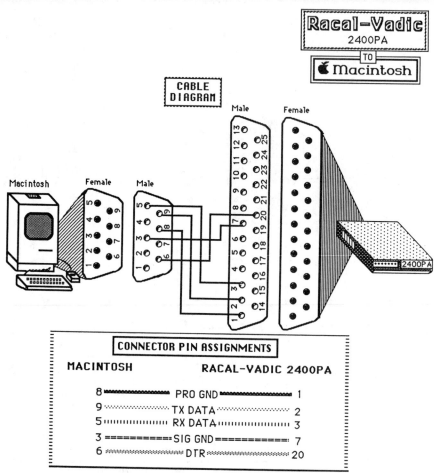

Racal-Vadic
2400PA
TO
 Macintosh

CABLE DIAGRAM

CONNECTOR PIN ASSIGNMENTS

MACINTOSH		RACAL-VADIC 2400PA
8	PRO GND	1
9	TX DATA	2
5	RX DATA	3
3	SIG GND	7
6	DTR	20

THERE ARE NO SWITCHES ON THIS MODEM. REFER TO
USER'S MANUAL FOR DISCUSSION OF OPTIONAL SETTINGS
IN NON-VOLATILE MEMORY. THE MODEM WILL WORK WITH
MANY SOFTWARE PACKAGES IN THE STANDARD CONFIGURA-
TION. FOR SOME PACKAGES OPTION 3 SHOULD BE SET TO 1.

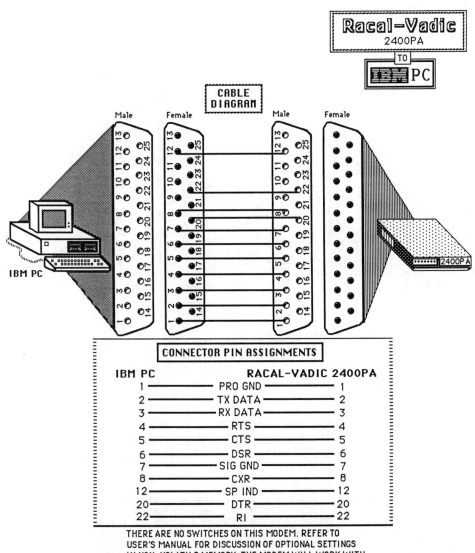

CABLE DIAGRAM

Racal-Vadic 2400PA TO IBM PC

CONNECTOR PIN ASSIGNMENTS

IBM PC		RACAL-VADIC 2400PA
1	PRO GND	1
2	TX DATA	2
3	RX DATA	3
4	RTS	4
5	CTS	5
6	DSR	6
7	SIG GND	7
8	CXR	8
12	SP IND	12
20	DTR	20
22	RI	22

THERE ARE NO SWITCHES ON THIS MODEM. REFER TO
USER'S MANUAL FOR DISCUSSION OF OPTIONAL SETTINGS
IN NON-VOLATILE MEMORY. THE MODEM WILL WORK WITH
MANY SOFTWARE PACKAGES IN THE STANDARD CONFIGURA-
TION. FOR SOME PACKAGES OPTION 3 SHOULD BE SET TO 1.

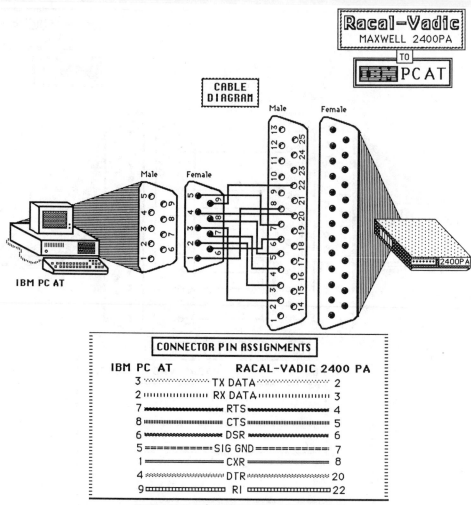

Racal-Vadic
MAXWELL 2400PA
TO
IBM PC AT

CABLE DIAGRAM

IBM PC AT

CONNECTOR PIN ASSIGNMENTS

IBM PC AT		RACAL-VADIC 2400 PA
3	TX DATA	2
2	RX DATA	3
7	RTS	4
8	CTS	5
6	DSR	6
5	SIG GND	7
1	CXR	8
4	DTR	20
9	RI	22

THERE ARE NO SWITCHES ON THIS MODEM. REFER TO
USER'S MANUAL FOR DISCUSSION OF OPTIONAL SETTINGS
IN NON-VOLATILE MEMORY. THE MODEM WILL WORK WITH
MANY SOFTWARE PACKAGES IN THE STANDARD CONFIGURA-
TION. FOR SOME PACKAGES OPTION 3 SHOULD BE SET TO 1.

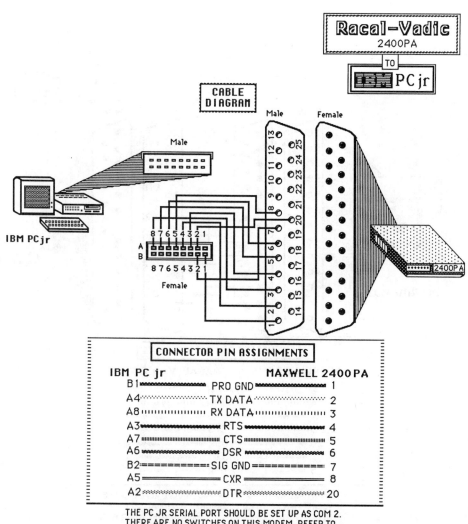

Racal–Vadic
2400PA

TO

IBM PC jr

CABLE DIAGRAM

IBM PCjr

CONNECTOR PIN ASSIGNMENTS

IBM PC jr		MAXWELL 2400PA
B1	PRO GND	1
A4	TX DATA	2
A8	RX DATA	3
A3	RTS	4
A7	CTS	5
A6	DSR	6
B2	SIG GND	7
A5	CXR	8
A2	DTR	20

THE PC JR SERIAL PORT SHOULD BE SET UP AS COM 2.
THERE ARE NO SWITCHES ON THIS MODEM. REFER TO
USER'S MANUAL FOR DISCUSSION OF OPTIONAL SETTINGS
IN NON-VOLATILE MEMORY. THE MODEM WILL WORK WITH
MANY SOFTWARE PACKAGES IN THE STANDARD CONFIGURA-
TION. FOR SOME PACKAGES OPTION 3 SHOULD BE SET TO 1.

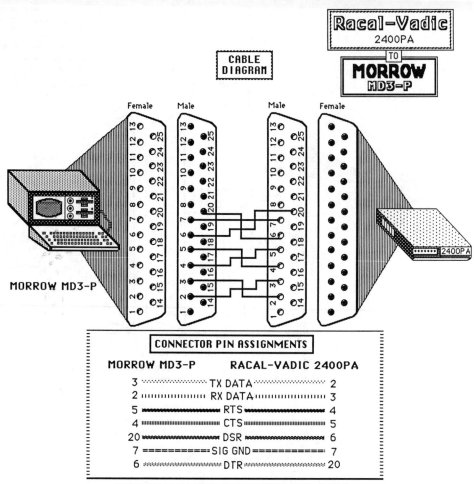

CABLE DIAGRAM

Racal-Vadic 2400PA TO **MORROW MD3-P**

Female Male Male Female

MORROW MD3-P

2400PA

CONNECTOR PIN ASSIGNMENTS		
MORROW MD3-P		RACAL-VADIC 2400PA
3	TX DATA	2
2	RX DATA	3
5	RTS	4
4	CTS	5
20	DSR	6
7	SIG GND	7
6	DTR	20

THERE ARE NO SWITCHES ON THIS MODEM. REFER TO THE
USER'S MANUAL FOR DISCUSSION OF OPTIONAL SETTINGS
IN NON-VOLATILE MEMORY. THE MODEM WILL WORK WITH
MANY SOFTWARE PACKAGES IN THE STANDARD CONFIGURA-
TION. FOR SOME PACKAGES OPTION 3 SHOULD BE SET TO 1.
THESE PINOUTS ARE FOR A SERIAL PORT IN THE STANDARD
CONFIGURATION.

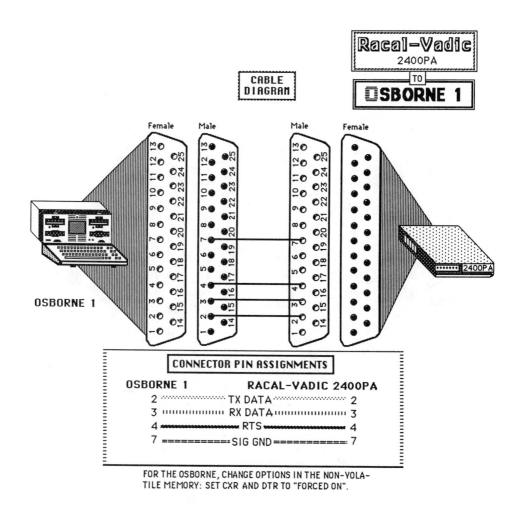

CABLE DIAGRAM

Racal-Vadic 2400PA
TO
OSBORNE 1

Female Male Male Female

OSBORNE 1

CONNECTOR PIN ASSIGNMENTS

OSBORNE 1		RACAL-VADIC 2400PA
2	TX DATA	2
3	RX DATA	3
4	RTS	4
7	SIG GND	7

FOR THE OSBORNE, CHANGE OPTIONS IN THE NON-VOLA-
TILE MEMORY: SET CXR AND DTR TO "FORCED ON".

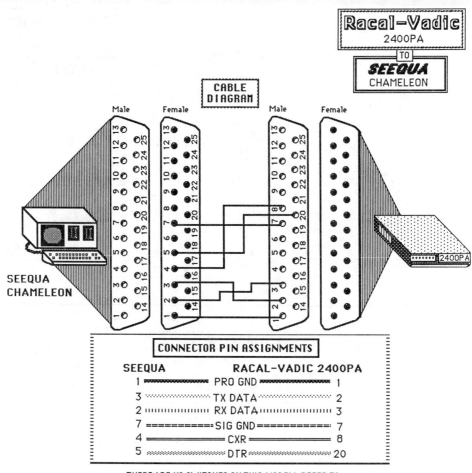

CABLE DIAGRAM

Racal-Vadic 2400PA TO SEEQUA CHAMELEON

SEEQUA CHAMELEON

CONNECTOR PIN ASSIGNMENTS

SEEQUA		RACAL-VADIC 2400PA
1	PRO GND	1
3	TX DATA	2
2	RX DATA	3
7	SIG GND	7
4	CXR	8
5	DTR	20

THERE ARE NO SWITCHES ON THIS MODEM. REFER TO USER'S MANUAL FOR DISCUSSION OF OPTIONAL SETTINGS IN NON-VOLATILE MEMORY. THE MODEM WILL WORK WITH MANY SOFTWARE PACKAGES IN THE STANDARD CONFIGURATION. FOR SOME PACKAGES OPTION 3 SHOULD BE SET TO 1.

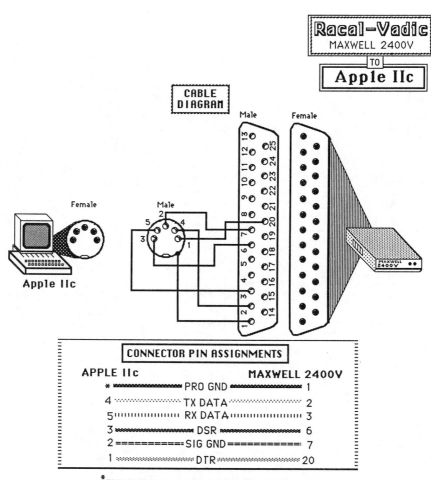

Racal-Vadic
MAXWELL 2400V
TO
Apple IIc

CABLE DIAGRAM

Female

Apple IIc

Male

Male

Female

CONNECTOR PIN ASSIGNMENTS

APPLE IIc		MAXWELL 2400V
*	PRO GND	1
4	TX DATA	2
5	RX DATA	3
3	DSR	6
2	SIG GND	7
1	DTR	20

*THIS LINE GOES TO THE DIN CONNECTOR SHELL.
THERE ARE NO SWITCHES ON THIS MODEM. IT IS
PRE-CONFIGURED FOR PC USERS. REFER TO USER'S
MANUAL FOR DISCUSSION OF OPTIONAL SETTINGS.
THIS MODEM WILL AUTODIAL USING RACAL-VADIC OR
HAYES COMMAND SETS.

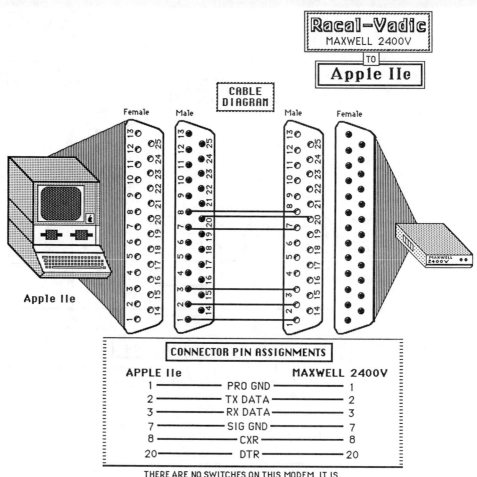

Racal-Vadic
MAXWELL 2400V
TO
Apple IIe

CABLE DIAGRAM

Apple IIe

CONNECTOR PIN ASSIGNMENTS

APPLE IIe		MAXWELL 2400V
1	PRO GND	1
2	TX DATA	2
3	RX DATA	3
7	SIG GND	7
8	CXR	8
20	DTR	20

THERE ARE NO SWITCHES ON THIS MODEM. IT IS
PRE-CONFIGURED FOR PC USERS. REFER TO USER'S
MANUAL FOR DISCUSSION OF OPTIONAL SETTINGS.
THIS MODEM WILL AUTODIAL USING RACAL-VADIC OR
HAYES COMMAND SETS.

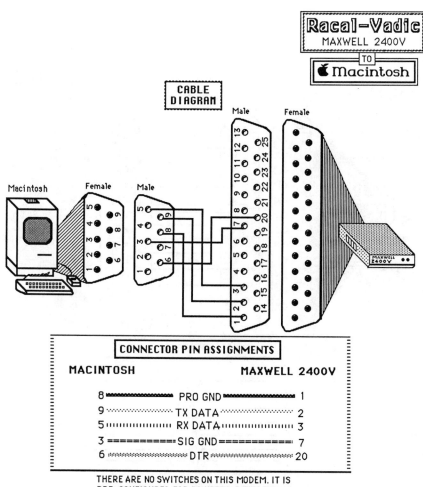

THERE ARE NO SWITCHES ON THIS MODEM. IT IS
PRE-CONFIGURED FOR PC USERS. REFER TO USER'S
MANUAL FOR DISCUSSION OF OPTIONAL SETTINGS.
THIS MODEM WILL AUTODIAL USING RACAL-VADIC OR
HAYES COMMAND SETS. JUMPER PINS 5 & 8 ON THE
MODEM END OF THE CABLE.

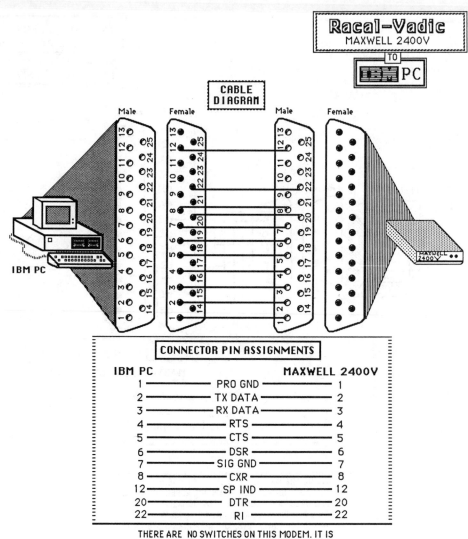

CABLE DIAGRAM

Racal-Vadic
MAXWELL 2400V
TO
IBM PC

Male Female Male Female

IBM PC

IBM PC		MAXWELL 2400V
1	PRO GND	1
2	TX DATA	2
3	RX DATA	3
4	RTS	4
5	CTS	5
6	DSR	6
7	SIG GND	7
8	CXR	8
12	SP IND	12
20	DTR	20
22	RI	22

CONNECTOR PIN ASSIGNMENTS

THERE ARE NO SWITCHES ON THIS MODEM. IT IS
PRE-CONFIGURED FOR PC USERS. REFER TO USER'S
MANUAL FOR DISCUSSION OF OPTIONAL SETTINGS.
THIS MODEM WILL AUTODIAL USING EITHER RACAL-
VADIC OR HAYES COMMANDS.

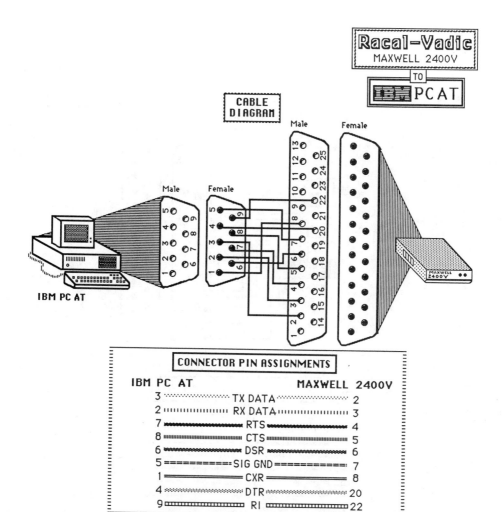

CABLE DIAGRAM

Racal-Vadic MAXWELL 2400V **TO** IBM PC AT

IBM PC AT

CONNECTOR PIN ASSIGNMENTS

IBM PC AT		MAXWELL 2400V
3	TX DATA	2
2	RX DATA	3
7	RTS	4
8	CTS	5
6	DSR	6
5	SIG GND	7
1	CXR	8
4	DTR	20
9	RI	22

THERE ARE NO SWITCHES ON THIS MODEM. IT IS
PRE-CONFIGURED FOR PC USERS. REFER TO USER'S
MANUAL FOR DISCUSSION OF OPTIONAL SETTINGS.
THIS MODEM WILL AUTODIAL USING RACAL-VADIC OR
HAYES COMMAND SETS.

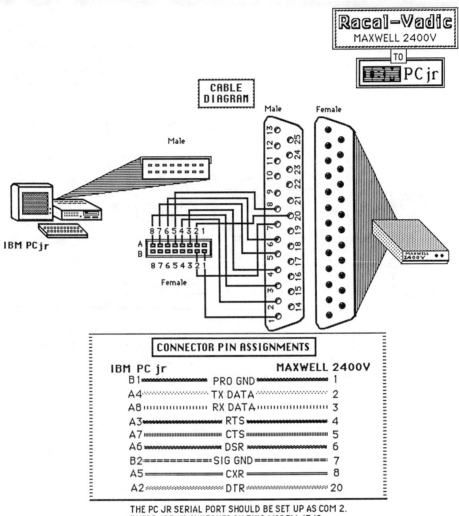

Racal-Vadic
MAXWELL 2400V
TO
IBM PC jr

CABLE
DIAGRAM

Male

Male

IBM PCjr

Female

Male   Female

MAXWELL
2400V

CONNECTOR PIN ASSIGNMENTS

IBM PC jr   MAXWELL 2400V
B1 ～～～～～～～ PRO GND ～～～～～～～ 1
A4 ·············· TX DATA ·············· 2
A8 |||||||||||||| RX DATA |||||||||||||| 3
A3 ▬▬▬▬▬▬▬ RTS ▬▬▬▬▬▬▬ 4
A7 ||||||||||||||| CTS ||||||||||||||| 5
A6 ～～～～～～～ DSR ～～～～～～～ 6
B2 ============ SIG GND ============ 7
A5 ──────────── CXR ──────────── 8
A2 ～～～～～～～ DTR ～～～～～～～ 20

THE PC JR SERIAL PORT SHOULD BE SET UP AS COM 2.
THERE ARE NO SWITCHES ON THIS MODEM. IT IS
PRE-CONFIGURED FOR PC USERS. REFER TO USER'S
MANUAL FOR DISCUSSION OF OPTIONAL SETTINGS.
THIS MODEM WILL AUTODIAL USING RACAL-VADIC OR
HAYES COMMAND SETS.

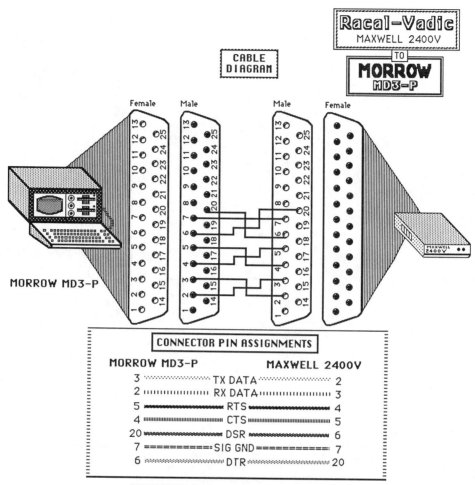

CABLE DIAGRAM

Racal-Vadic
MAXWELL 2400V
TO
MORROW MD3-P

Female Male Male Female

MORROW MD3-P

CONNECTOR PIN ASSIGNMENTS

MORROW MD3-P   MAXWELL 2400V

3	TX DATA	2
2	RX DATA	3
5	RTS	4
4	CTS	5
20	DSR	6
7	SIG GND	7
6	DTR	20

THERE ARE NO SWITCHES ON THIS MODEM. IT IS
PRE-CONFIGURED FOR PC USERS. REFER TO USER'S
MANUAL FOR DISCUSSION OF OPTIONAL SETTINGS.
THIS MODEM WILL AUTODIAL USING RACAL-VADIC
OR HAYES COMMAND SETS. THESE PINOUTS ARE FOR
A SERIAL PORT IN THE STANDARD CONFIGURATION.

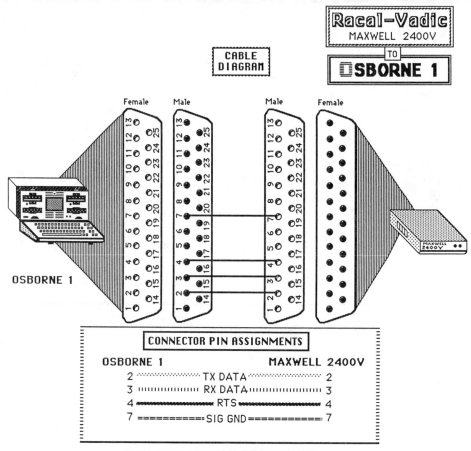

CABLE DIAGRAM

Racal-Vadic
MAXWELL 2400V
TO
OSBORNE 1

Female   Male   Male   Female

OSBORNE 1

CONNECTOR PIN ASSIGNMENTS

OSBORNE 1   MAXWELL 2400V
2 .... TX DATA 2
3 |||||||||||||| RX DATA |||||||||||||||||| 3
4 ━━━━━━━━━━ RTS ━━━━━━━━━━━━ 4
7 =========== SIG GND =========== 7

THERE ARE NO SWITCHES ON THIS MODEM. IT IS
PRE-CONFIGURED FOR PC USERS. REFER TO USER'S
MANUAL FOR DISCUSSION OF OPTIONAL SETTINGS.
THIS MODEM WILL AUTODIAL USING RACAL-VADIC OR
HAYES COMMAND SETS. THE OSBORNE DOESN'T RAISE
DTR HIGH SO THIS SIGNAL MUST BE FORCED AT THE
MODEM END. SEE USER'S MANUAL FOR DETAILS.

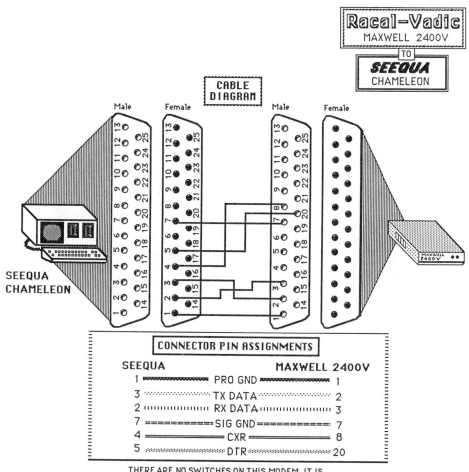

Racal-Vadic
MAXWELL 2400V
TO
SEEQUA
CHAMELEON

CABLE DIAGRAM

Male   Female   Male   Female

SEEQUA
CHAMELEON

CONNECTOR PIN ASSIGNMENTS

SEEQUA		MAXWELL 2400V
1	PRO GND	1
3	TX DATA	2
2	RX DATA	3
7	SIG GND	7
4	CXR	8
5	DTR	20

THERE ARE NO SWITCHES ON THIS MODEM. IT IS
PRE-CONFIGURED FOR PC USERS. REFER TO USER'S
MANUAL FOR DISCUSSION OF OPTIONAL SETTINGS.
THIS MODEM WILL AUTODIAL USING RACAL-VADIC OR
HAYES COMMAND SETS.

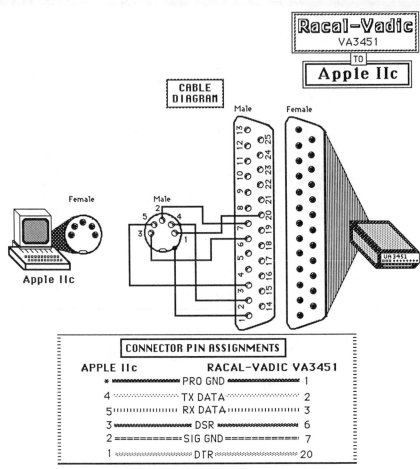

Racal-Vadic
VA3451

TO

Apple IIc

CABLE DIAGRAM

Female

Male

Apple IIc

CONNECTOR PIN ASSIGNMENTS

APPLE IIc		RACAL-VADIC VA3451
*	PRO GND	1
4	TX DATA	2
5	RX DATA	3
3	DSR	6
2	SIG GND	7
1	DTR	20

*THIS LINE GOES TO THE DIN CONNECTOR SHELL.
SEE USER'S MANUAL FOR STRAP OPTION INSTRUCTIONS.
GENERALLY FOR PC APPLICATIONS IT IS BEST TO STRAP
CXR NORMAL AND DTR TO BE UNDER TERMINAL CONTROL.
IF YOU WISH TO AUTODIAL, BE SURE THAT YOU HAVE A
MODEM WITH THE AUTODIAL OPTION. A SOFTWARE THAT
IS TAILORED TO AUTODIAL THIS MODEM IS RACAL-VADIC'S
GEORGE V 2.0.

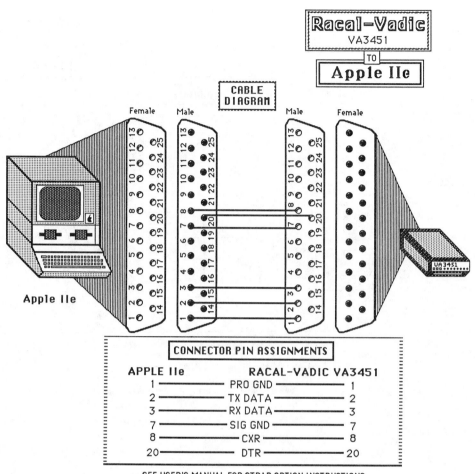

Racal-Vadic
VA3451
TO
Apple IIe

CABLE DIAGRAM

Female   Male   Male   Female

Apple IIe

CONNECTOR PIN ASSIGNMENTS

APPLE IIe		RACAL-VADIC VA3451
1	PRO GND	1
2	TX DATA	2
3	RX DATA	3
7	SIG GND	7
8	CXR	8
20	DTR	20

SEE USER'S MANUAL FOR STRAP OPTION INSTRUCTIONS.
GENERALLY FOR PC APPLICATIONS IT IS BEST TO STRAP
CXR NORMAL AND DTR TO BE UNDER TERMINAL CONTROL.
IF YOU WISH TO AUTODIAL, BE SURE THAT YOU HAVE A
MODEM WITH THE AUTODIAL OPTION. A SOFTWARE THAT
IS TAILORED TO AUTODIAL THIS MODEM IS RACAL-VADIC'S
GEORGE V 2.0 .

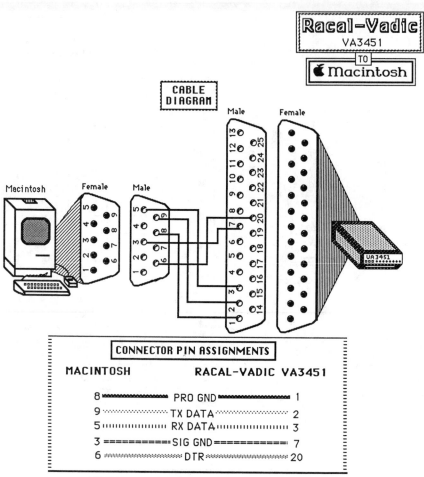

CABLE DIAGRAM

Racal-Vadic VA3451 TO Macintosh

CONNECTOR PIN ASSIGNMENTS

MACINTOSH		RACAL-VADIC VA3451
8	PRO GND	1
9	TX DATA	2
5	RX DATA	3
3	SIG GND	7
6	DTR	20

SEE USER'S MANUAL FOR STRAP OPTION INSTRUCTIONS. GENERALLY FOR PC APPLICATIONS IT IS BEST TO STRAP CXR NORMAL AND DTR TO BE UNDER TERMINAL CONTROL. IF YOU WISH TO AUTODIAL, BE SURE THAT YOU HAVE A MODEM WITH THE AUTODIAL OPTION. A SOFTWARE THAT IS TAILORED TO AUTODIAL THIS MODEM IS RACAL-VADIC'S *MACGEORGE*.

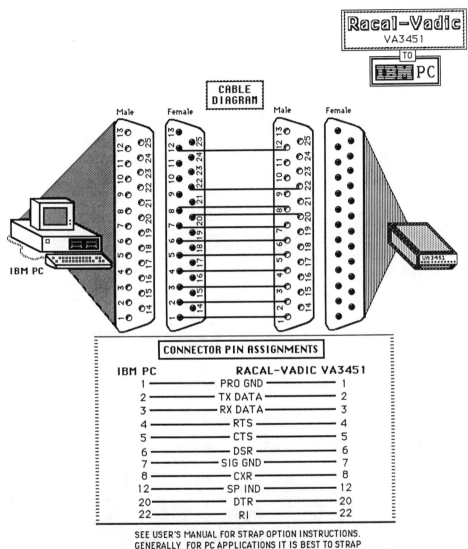

CABLE DIAGRAM

Racal-Vadic VA3451 TO IBM PC

CONNECTOR PIN ASSIGNMENTS

IBM PC		RACAL-VADIC VA3451
1	PRO GND	1
2	TX DATA	2
3	RX DATA	3
4	RTS	4
5	CTS	5
6	DSR	6
7	SIG GND	7
8	CXR	8
12	SP IND	12
20	DTR	20
22	RI	22

SEE USER'S MANUAL FOR STRAP OPTION INSTRUCTIONS.
GENERALLY FOR PC APPLICATIONS IT IS BEST TO STRAP
CXR NORMAL AND DTR TO BE UNDER TERMINAL CONTROL.
IF YOU WISH TO AUTODIAL, BE SURE THAT YOU HAVE A
MODEM WITH THE AUTODIAL OPTION. A SOFTWARE THAT
IS TAILORED TO AUTODIAL THIS MODEM IS RACAL-VADIC'S
GEORGE V 2.0 .

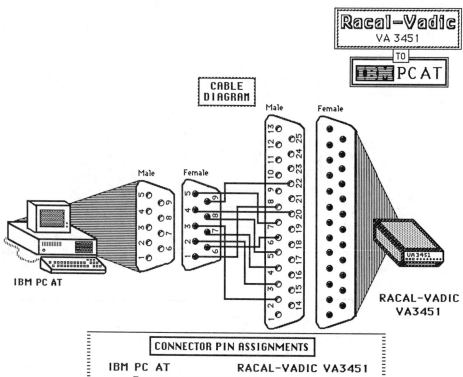

Racal-Vadic VA 3451
TO
IBM PC AT

CABLE DIAGRAM

IBM PC AT

RACAL-VADIC VA3451

CONNECTOR PIN ASSIGNMENTS		
IBM PC AT		**RACAL-VADIC VA3451**
3	TX DATA	2
2	RX DATA	3
7	RTS	4
8	CTS	5
6	DSR	6
5	SIG GND	7
1	CXR	8
4	DTR	20
9	RI	22

SEE USER'S MANUAL FOR STRAP OPTION INSTRUCTIONS.
GENERALLY, FOR PC APPLICATIONS IT IS BEST TO STRAP
CXR NORMAL AND DTR TO BE UNDER TERMINAL CONTROL.
IF YOU WISH TO AUTODIAL, BE SURE THAT YOU HAVE A
MODEM WITH THE AUTODIAL OPTION. A SOFTWARE THAT
IS TAILORED TO AUTODIAL THIS MODEM IS RACAL-VADIC'S
GEORGE V 2.0.

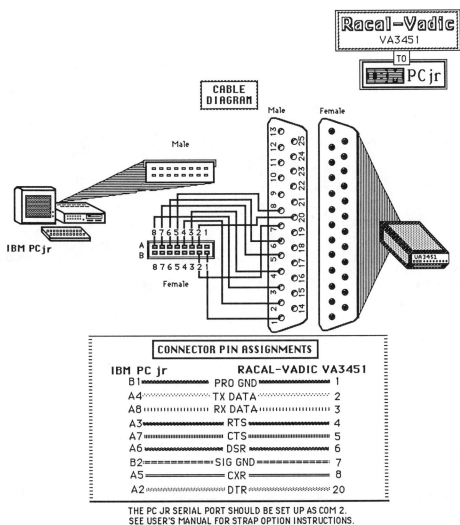

CABLE DIAGRAM

Racal-Vadic
VA3451
TO
IBM PCjr

Male

Female

Male

IBM PCjr

Female

VA3451

CONNECTOR PIN ASSIGNMENTS

IBM PC jr		RACAL-VADIC VA3451
B1	PRO GND	1
A4	TX DATA	2
A8	RX DATA	3
A3	RTS	4
A7	CTS	5
A6	DSR	6
B2	SIG GND	7
A5	CXR	8
A2	DTR	20

THE PC JR SERIAL PORT SHOULD BE SET UP AS COM 2.
SEE USER'S MANUAL FOR STRAP OPTION INSTRUCTIONS.
GENERALLY FOR PC APPLICATIONS IT IS BEST TO STRAP
CXR NORMAL AND DTR TO BE UNDER TERMINAL CONTROL.
IF YOU WISH TO AUTODIAL, BE SURE THAT YOU HAVE A
MODEM WITH THE AUTODIAL OPTION. A SOFTWARE THAT
IS TAILORED TO AUTODIAL THIS MODEM IS RACAL-VADIC'S
GEORGE V 2.0.

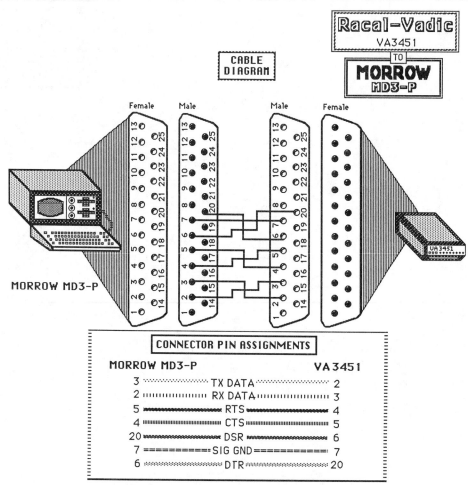

CABLE DIAGRAM

Racal-Vadic VA3451 TO MORROW MD3-P

Female   Male   Male   Female

MORROW MD3-P

CONNECTOR PIN ASSIGNMENTS

MORROW MD3-P   VA 3451

3	~~~~~~~~~ TX DATA ~~~~~~~~~	2
2	.... RX DATA	3
5	RTS	4
4	CTS	5
20	DSR	6
7	========== SIG GND ==========	7
6	DTR	20

SEE USER'S MANUAL FOR STRAP OPTION INSTRUCTIONS.
GENERALLY FOR PC APPLICATIONS IT IS BEST TO STRAP
CXR NORMAL AND DTR TO BE UNDER TERMINAL CONTROL.
IF YOU WISH TO AUTODIAL, BE SURE THAT YOU HAVE A
MODEM WITH THE AUTODIAL OPTION. THESE PINOUTS ARE
FOR A SERIAL PORT IN THE STANDARD CONFIGURATION.

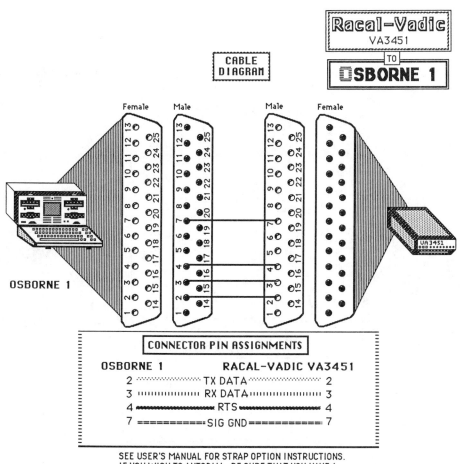

CABLE DIAGRAM

Racal–Vadic VA3451
TO
OSBORNE 1

Female   Male   Male   Female

OSBORNE 1

CONNECTOR PIN ASSIGNMENTS

OSBORNE 1		RACAL-VADIC VA3451
2	TX DATA	2
3	RX DATA	3
4	RTS	4
7	SIG GND	7

SEE USER'S MANUAL FOR STRAP OPTION INSTRUCTIONS.
IF YOU WISH TO AUTODIAL, BE SURE THAT YOU HAVE A
MODEM WITH THE AUTODIAL OPTION. FOR THE OSBORNE,
STRAP DTR AND CXR HIGH.

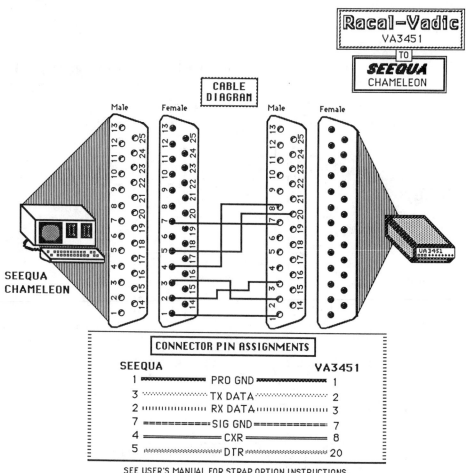

Racal-Vadic
VA3451
TO
SEEQUA
CHAMELEON

CABLE DIAGRAM

Male   Female   Male   Female

SEEQUA
CHAMELEON

VA3451

CONNECTOR PIN ASSIGNMENTS

SEEQUA		VA3451
1	PRO GND	1
3	TX DATA	2
2	RX DATA	3
7	SIG GND	7
4	CXR	8
5	DTR	20

SEE USER'S MANUAL FOR STRAP OPTION INSTRUCTIONS.
GENERALLY FOR PC APPLICATIONS IT IS BEST TO STRAP
CXR NORMAL AND DTR TO BE UNDER TERMINAL CONTROL.
IF YOU WISH TO AUTODIAL, BE SURE THAT YOU HAVE A
MODEM WITH THE AUTODIAL OPTION. A SOFTWARE THAT
IS TAILORED TO AUTODIAL THIS MODEM IS RACAL-VADIC'S
GEORGE V 2.0.

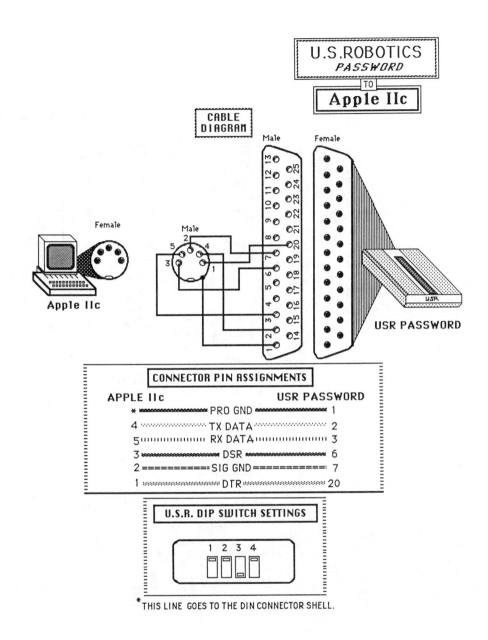

U.S.ROBOTICS
PASSWORD
[TO]
Apple IIc

CABLE DIAGRAM

Male   Female

Female

Apple IIc

Male

USR PASSWORD

CONNECTOR PIN ASSIGNMENTS

APPLE IIc   USR PASSWORD
* ~~~~~~~~~~~~~~~~ PRO GND ~~~~~~~~~~~~~~~~ 1
4 ~~~~~~~~~~~~~~ TX DATA ~~~~~~~~~~~~~ 2
5 ||||||||||||||||| RX DATA ||||||||||||||||| 3
3 ~~~~~~~~~~~~~~~~ DSR ~~~~~~~~~~~~~~~~ 6
2 ============ SIG GND ============ 7
1 ~~~~~~~~~~~~~~~~ DTR ~~~~~~~~~~~~~~~~ 20

U.S.R. DIP SWITCH SETTINGS

1 2 3 4

*THIS LINE GOES TO THE DIN CONNECTOR SHELL.

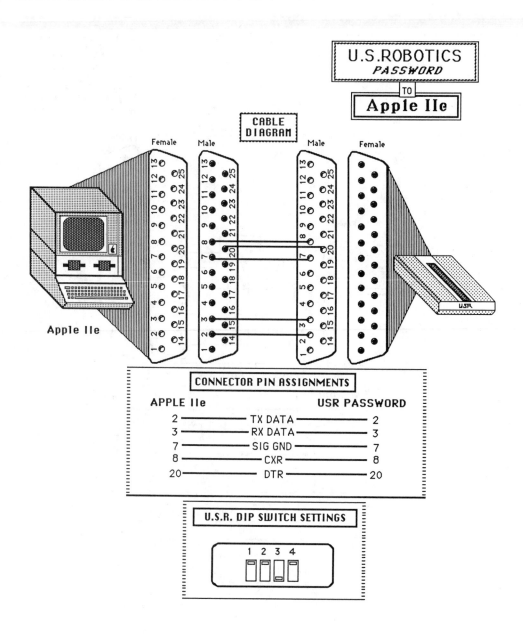

U.S.ROBOTICS
PASSWORD

TO

Apple IIe

CABLE DIAGRAM

CONNECTOR PIN ASSIGNMENTS

APPLE IIe		USR PASSWORD
2 ————	TX DATA ————	2
3 ————	RX DATA ————	3
7 ————	SIG GND ————	7
8 ————	CXR ————	8
20 ————	DTR ————	20

U.S.R. DIP SWITCH SETTINGS

1 2 3 4

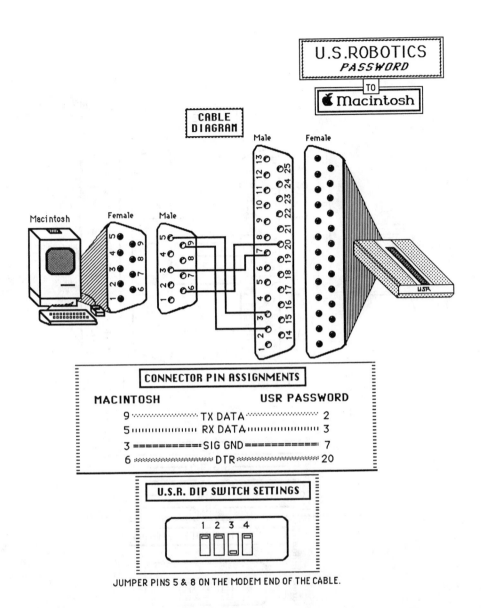

JUMPER PINS 5 & 8 ON THE MODEM END OF THE CABLE.

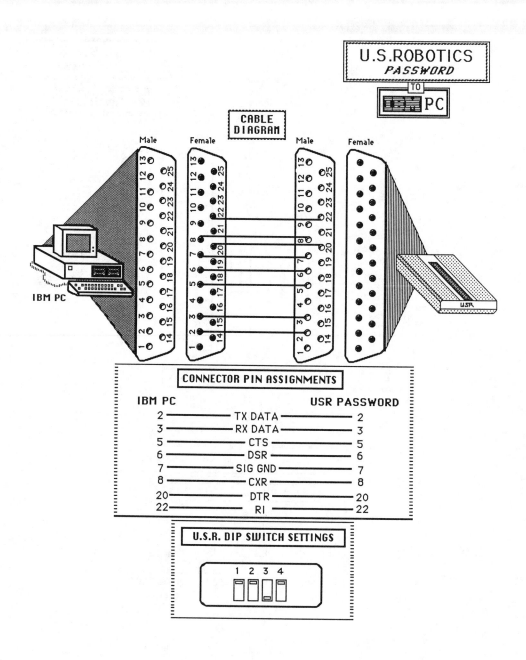

U.S.ROBOTICS
PASSWORD

TO

IBM PC

CABLE
DIAGRAM

CONNECTOR PIN ASSIGNMENTS

IBM PC   USR PASSWORD

2 ————————— TX DATA ————————— 2
3 ————————— RX DATA ————————— 3
5 ————————————— CTS ————————————— 5
6 ————————————— DSR ————————————— 6
7 ————————— SIG GND ————————— 7
8 ————————————— CXR ————————————— 8
20 ————————————— DTR ————————————— 20
22 ————————————— RI ————————————— 22

U.S.R. DIP SWITCH SETTINGS

1 2 3 4

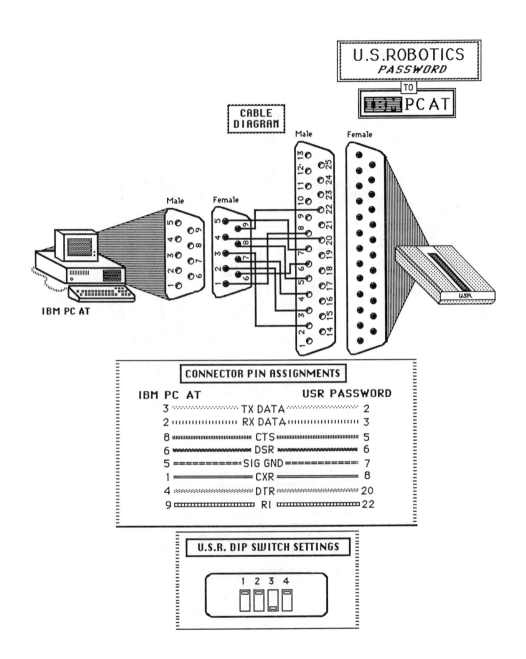

U.S.ROBOTICS *PASSWORD*

TO

IBM PC AT

CABLE DIAGRAM

Male

Female

Male

Female

IBM PC AT

CONNECTOR PIN ASSIGNMENTS

IBM PC AT		USR PASSWORD
3	TX DATA	2
2	RX DATA	3
8	CTS	5
6	DSR	6
5	SIG GND	7
1	CXR	8
4	DTR	20
9	RI	22

U.S.R. DIP SWITCH SETTINGS

1 2 3 4

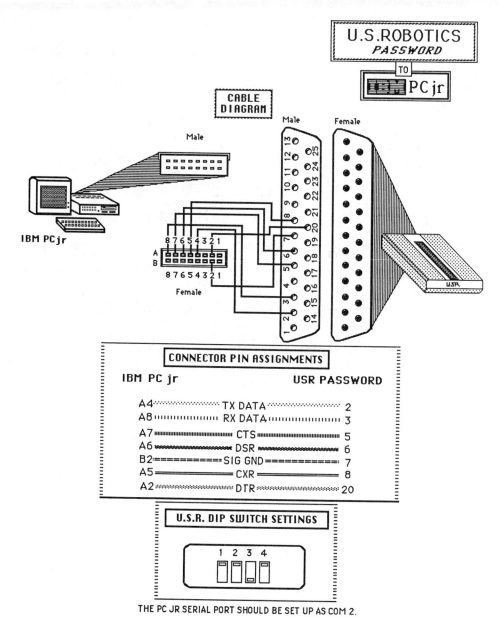

CABLE DIAGRAM

Male

Male

Female

IBM PCjr

A
B

87654321

87654321

Female

U.S.ROBOTICS
PASSWORD

TO

IBM PCjr

CONNECTOR PIN ASSIGNMENTS

IBM PC jr   USR PASSWORD

A4 ··················· TX DATA ··················· 2
A8 ‖‖‖‖‖‖‖‖‖‖ RX DATA ‖‖‖‖‖‖‖‖‖‖ 3
A7 ▬▬▬▬▬▬▬ CTS ▬▬▬▬▬▬▬ 5
A6 〜〜〜〜〜〜 DSR 〜〜〜〜〜〜 6
B2 ========= SIG GND ========= 7
A5 ━━━━━━━ CXR ━━━━━━━ 8
A2 〜〜〜〜〜〜 DTR 〜〜〜〜〜〜 20

U.S.R. DIP SWITCH SETTINGS

1 2 3 4

THE PC JR SERIAL PORT SHOULD BE SET UP AS COM 2.

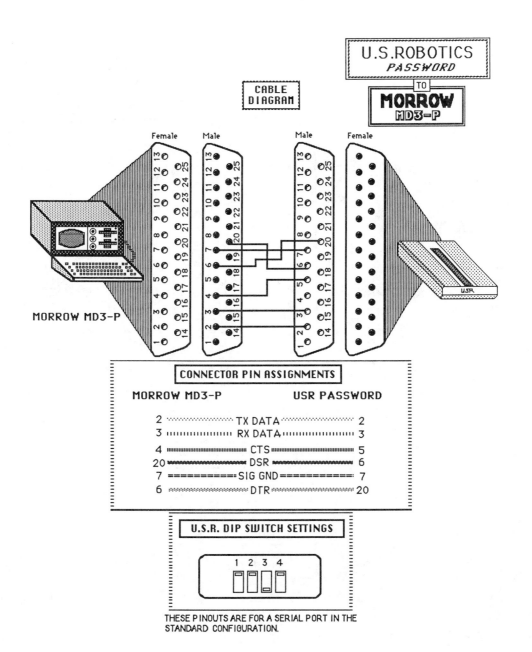

CABLE DIAGRAM

U.S.ROBOTICS *PASSWORD*

TO

MORROW MD3-P

Female   Male   Male   Female

MORROW MD3-P

CONNECTOR PIN ASSIGNMENTS

MORROW MD3-P   USR PASSWORD

2	TX DATA	2
3	RX DATA	3
4	CTS	5
20	DSR	6
7	SIG GND	7
6	DTR	20

U.S.R. DIP SWITCH SETTINGS

1 2 3 4

THESE PINOUTS ARE FOR A SERIAL PORT IN THE
STANDARD CONFIGURATION.

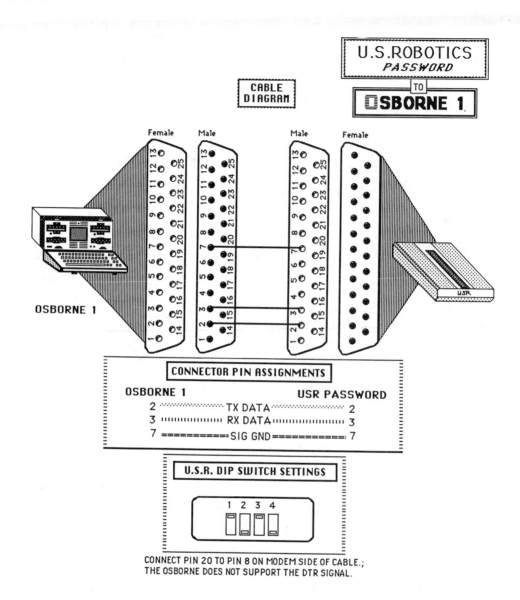

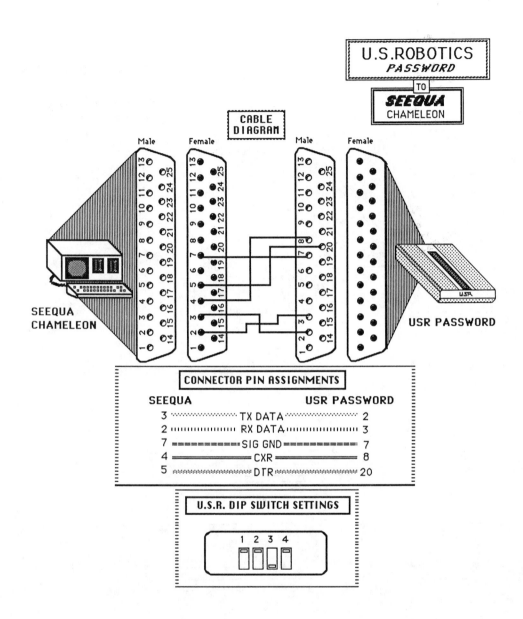

U.S.ROBOTICS
PASSWORD
TO
SEEQUA
CHAMELEON

CABLE DIAGRAM

CONNECTOR PIN ASSIGNMENTS

SEEQUA		USR PASSWORD
3	TX DATA	2
2	RX DATA	3
7	SIG GND	7
4	CXR	8
5	DTR	20

U.S.R. DIP SWITCH SETTINGS

1 2 3 4

ANCHOR AUTOMATION
VOLKSMODEM 12
TO
Apple IIc

CABLE
DIAGRAM

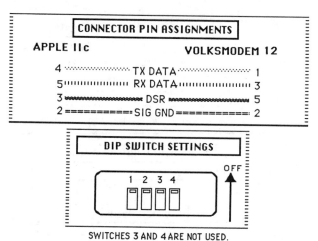

Female

Apple IIc

Male

Male

Female

CONNECTOR PIN ASSIGNMENTS

APPLE IIc   VOLKSMODEM 12

4 ················· TX DATA ················· 1
5'''''''''''''''' RX DATA '''''''''''''''' 3
3 ~~~~~~~~~~~~~ DSR ~~~~~~~~~~~~~ 5
2 ===========SIG GND=========== 2

DIP SWITCH SETTINGS

OFF

1 2 3 4

SWITCHES 3 AND 4 ARE NOT USED.

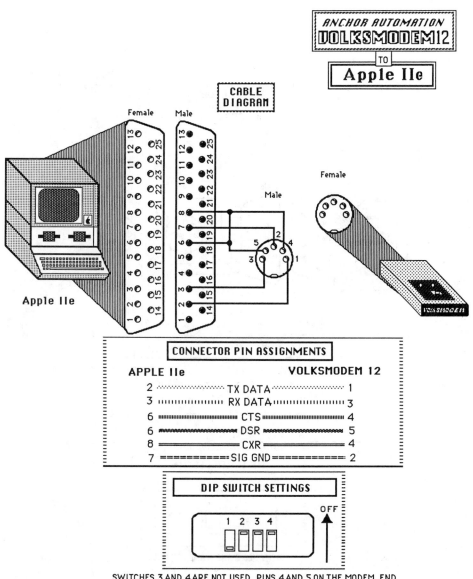

ANCHOR AUTOMATION
VOLKSMODEM 12
TO
Apple IIe

CABLE DIAGRAM

Female   Male

Female

Male

Apple IIe

CONNECTOR PIN ASSIGNMENTS

APPLE IIe   VOLKSMODEM 12

2	TX DATA	1
3	RX DATA	3
6	CTS	4
6	DSR	5
8	CXR	4
7	SIG GND	2

DIP SWITCH SETTINGS

OFF

1 2 3 4

SWITCHES 3 AND 4 ARE NOT USED. PINS 4 AND 5 ON THE MODEM END
OF THE CABLE ARE CONNECTED TOGETHER SINCE IIe DOESN'T SUPPORT
BOTH THOSE SIGNALS.

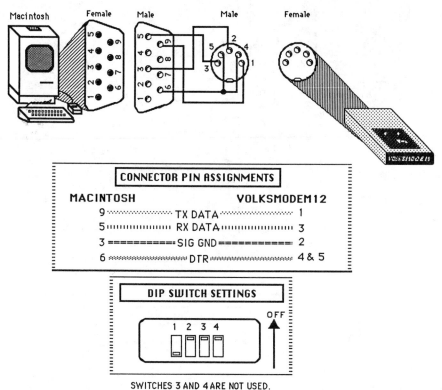

CABLE DIAGRAM

CONNECTOR PIN ASSIGNMENTS

MACINTOSH		VOLKSMODEM12
9	TX DATA	1
5	RX DATA	3
3	SIG GND	2
6	DTR	4 & 5

DIP SWITCH SETTINGS

OFF

1 2 3 4

SWITCHES 3 AND 4 ARE NOT USED.

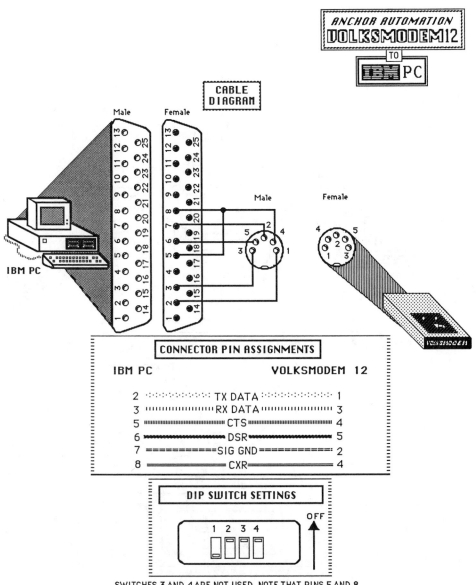

CABLE DIAGRAM

ANCHOR AUTOMATION VOLKSMODEM 12 TO IBM PC

CONNECTOR PIN ASSIGNMENTS

IBM PC		VOLKSMODEM 12
2	TX DATA	1
3	RX DATA	3
5	CTS	4
6	DSR	5
7	SIG GND	2
8	CXR	4

DIP SWITCH SETTINGS

OFF

1 2 3 4

SWITCHES 3 AND 4 ARE NOT USED. NOTE THAT PINS 5 AND 8 FROM THE PC ARE BOTH CONNECTED TO PIN 4 OF THE MODEM PLUG.

ANCHOR AUTOMATION
VOLKSMODEM 12
TO
IBM PC AT

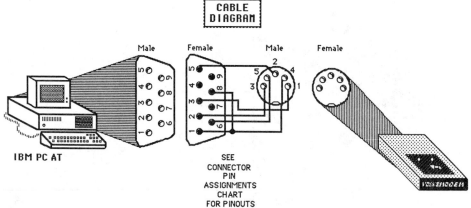

CABLE
DIAGRAM

Male   Female   Male   Female

IBM PC AT

SEE
CONNECTOR
PIN
ASSIGNMENTS
CHART
FOR PINOUTS

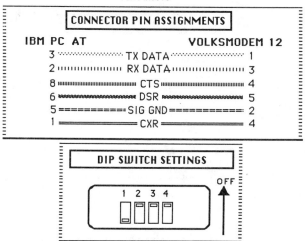

CONNECTOR PIN ASSIGNMENTS

IBM PC AT		VOLKSMODEM 12
3	TX DATA	1
2	RX DATA	3
8	CTS	4
6	DSR	5
5	SIG GND	2
1	CXR	4

DIP SWITCH SETTINGS

OFF

1 2 3 4

SWITCHES 3 AND 4 ARE NOT USED.
PIN 4 ON MODEM SIDE GOES TO TWO
PINS ON PC AT SIDE.

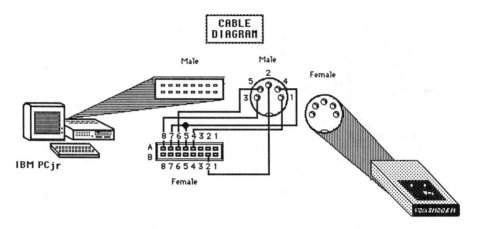

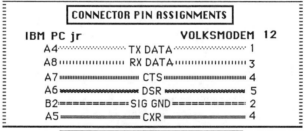

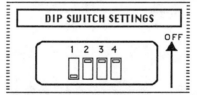

THE PC JR SERIAL PORT SHOULD BE SET UP AS COM 2. SWITCHES 3 AND 4 ARE NOT USED. NOTE THAT PINS A5 AND A7 FROM THE PC JR BOTH CONNECT TO PIN 4 OF THE VOLKSMODEM.

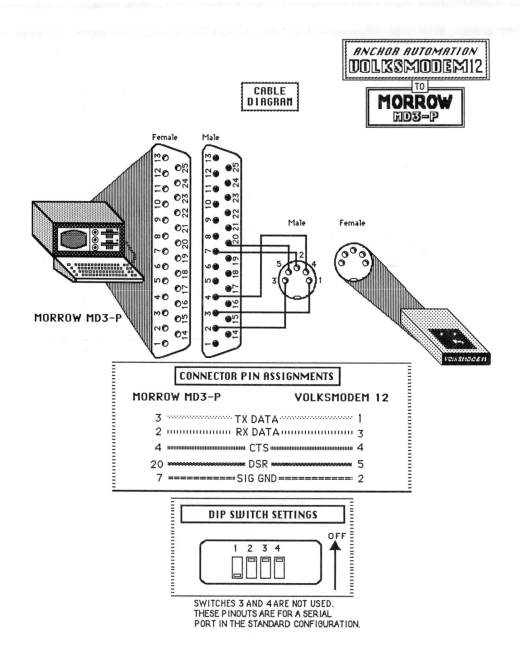

CABLE
DIAGRAM

ANCHOR AUTOMATION
VOLKSMODEM 12
TO
MORROW
MD3-P

CONNECTOR PIN ASSIGNMENTS

MORROW MD3-P   VOLKSMODEM 12

3	TX DATA	1
2	RX DATA	3
4	CTS	4
20	DSR	5
7	SIG GND	2

DIP SWITCH SETTINGS

OFF

1 2 3 4

SWITCHES 3 AND 4 ARE NOT USED.
THESE PINOUTS ARE FOR A SERIAL
PORT IN THE STANDARD CONFIGURATION.

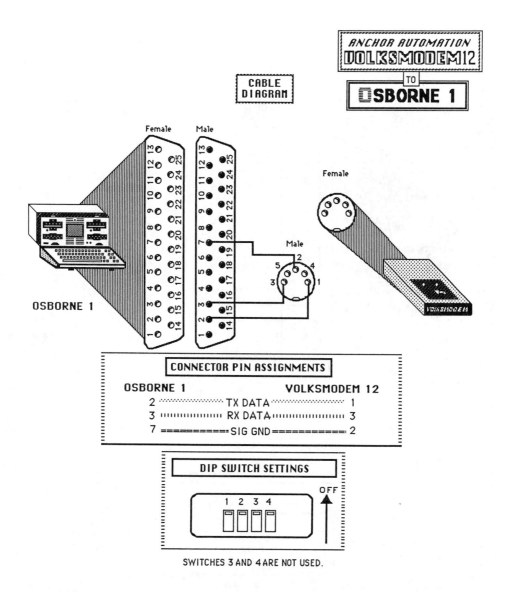

CABLE
DIAGRAM

ANCHOR AUTOMATION
VOLKSMODEM 12
TO
OSBORNE 1

Female   Male

Female

Male

OSBORNE 1

CONNECTOR PIN ASSIGNMENTS

OSBORNE 1   VOLKSMODEM 12

2 ·············· TX DATA ·············· 1
3 |||||||||||||| RX DATA |||||||||||||| 3
7 ============ SIG GND ============ 2

DIP SWITCH SETTINGS

1 2 3 4   OFF

SWITCHES 3 AND 4 ARE NOT USED.

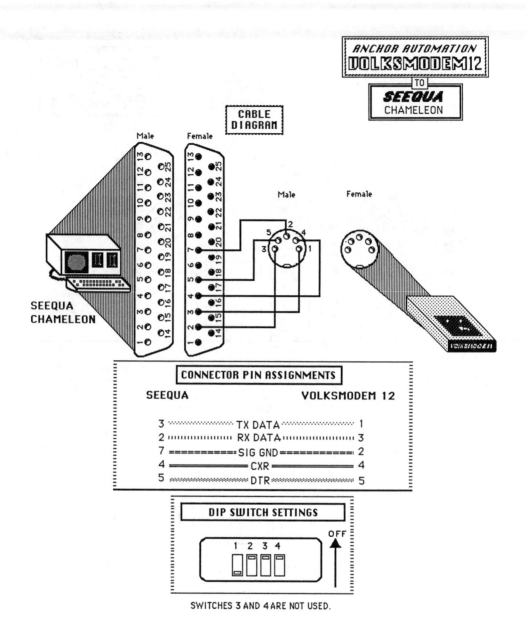

ANCHOR AUTOMATION
VOLKSMODEM 12
TO
SEEQUA
CHAMELEON

CABLE DIAGRAM

Male Female

Male Female

SEEQUA
CHAMELEON

CONNECTOR PIN ASSIGNMENTS

SEEQUA   VOLKSMODEM 12

3 ·········· TX DATA ·········· 1
2 ·········· RX DATA ·········· 3
7 ========= SIG GND ========= 2
4 ————————— CXR ————————— 4
5 ·········· DTR ·········· 5

DIP SWITCH SETTINGS

OFF

1 2 3 4

SWITCHES 3 AND 4 ARE NOT USED.

A

Call Me, Modem

The most exciting part of using a modem attached to a computer is your instant access to:

up-to-the-minute news of various kinds

information from millions of published pages: electronic library searches

thousands of people, most of whom you would be unlikely to meet and converse with any other way

instant mail

home banking, airline reservations, and ordering of consumer goods

For years we've been promised that the computer would bring all the knowledge of the world into our homes and offices, and this knowledge is finally coming within reach. The whole area of online services, networks, and data bases is exploding. These things are getting easier to use, more accessible, and may be getting cheaper.

Types of Online Services

The companies that provide this wonderful world of access used to be in clearly defined categories. A few well-known names are provided as examples.

Online services or information utilities: The Source, CompuServe, Dow Jones News/Retrieval Service (wire service news, stocks, airline information, electronic mailbox, party line or CB for free-form teleconferencing [so far, CompuServe only])

Online data bases: Dialog/Knowledge Index, BRS (Bibliographic Research Service) and BRS/After Dark, Mead Data Central (Nexis and Lexis), Newsnet, Orbit (access to specialized data bases, including those related to medicine, law, industrial chemistry, computer industry, and patent information)

Public electronic mail services: MCI, Easylink, (password-protected mailboxes for users, hard copy delivered by courier or U.S. mail, phone messaging service)

Free public bulletin boards: local systems usually based on interest groups with mail for users, calendars of events, software, goods and services advertised by users)

Today the online explosion is blurring these categories. For example, some online data bases are now offering mailboxes for users, and some electronic mail services are offering gateway service to data bases.

Home Banking

Some banks allow their customers to pay bills and otherwise transfer funds from their accounts to the accounts of businesses. Until 20 dollar bills can pop out of disk drives, this service will remain limited in popularity.

Data Bases

Online data bases have always seemed fairly expensive and difficult to use. The two major services, Dialog and BRS, responded in 1983 with evening and weekend service on smaller versions of themselves (Knowledge Index and BRS/After Dark, respectively) at much lower rates. These and other companies also have come out with "front end" software (Dialog's In-Search is an example) to expedite the search process.

Gateway Services

The command structure can be difficult to learn, but front end software tries to mitigate this difficulty. Another problem is getting a subscription to an online data base, which may take several weeks. Why can't the process be as easy as dialing a telephone number? Independent *gateway services* solve this problem. At present, two major services exist, each with a different approach: EasyNet and Business Computer Network.

EasyNet (not related to Western Union's Easylink) is easiest to access. Instead of mailing in a registration to an online data base and waiting for an ID and password, you simply dial 800-EASYNET via your modem. If you want to make a search, EasyNet asks for credit card information. After this information is entered and verified, simple menus help you narrow down your search topic. EasyNet then calls one of the big-name data bases (you may choose one or leave the choice up to EasyNet) and gets the information. Thus you are not faced with learning the intricacies of search commands for Dialog, NewsNet, or BRS. At this writing, charges are $6 for access and $6 for a search.

Business Computer Network's (BCN) low membership fee includes specialized communications software, SuperScout, which is the only way to log onto BCN. BCN offers more data bases than EasyNet. BCN is unique also in providing access to online utilities such as CompuServe.

Electronic Mailboxes

Another example of the way that the online world is becoming cheaper and easier to use is the electronic mailbox. This is one of the most used parts of online services like the Source and CompuServe or mail services like MCI Mail. As a way for people to get in touch, anyone in the computer industry, especially those who have published, routinely, lists their mailboxes on these services. However, cost puts national electronic mailboxes beyond the reach of a great number of people. As a result, low-cost local alternatives are springing up in the San Francisco Bay area, Colorado, Boston, Ann Arbor/Detroit, and Toronto that provide mailboxes at one-third to one-twelfth the fee charged by the national companies. By offering conference capability, these local services fall in between the national services and the free bulletin boards.

The online area is expanding and changing faster than any other area in the personal computer field. You can try to get up-to-date information on this subject from computer magazines, which tend to devote one issue a year to communications and occasionally publish something about what is available online. Annually updated directories of data bases are available also (see Appendix C, *Further Reading*.)

Bulletin Boards

Bulletin boards are a low-cost way to get your modem's "feet wet." For the cost of a local call, get experience in "roaming around" an online system. Bulletin boards (BBS) are analogous to the physical bulletin boards at your local laundromat or supermarket, but BBS usually have an audience extending far beyond a single neighborhood. Some boards have a national readership.

BBS are famous for offering free software for downloading, although many boards do not have any software. Many of those that do will ask a membership fee or otherwise charge for the service. Almost all boards have messages to read, and many let you post messages for free.

More and more specialized boards are springing into existence. In addition to boards that specialize (like computer user groups) in particular computer brands or operating systems or in games and other programs, you can find boards based on noncomputer interests, such as aviation, rock music, photography and motion pictures, health, the insurance industry, parenting, bicycling, short stories, or the peace movement.

How can you find out about free bulletin boards? Monthly national magazines devoted to specific computers, like *PC*, publish a list of bulletin boards and user groups broken down by state. In addition, most large urban areas will have one or more free tabloid computer newspapers, which list local boards and groups. These lists are usually pretty current. You can ask your dealer to supply local bulletin board numbers. Some stores have their own boards. If in-store boards or local numbers are not available, store personnel might be able to steer you to a user group with members who would know a few boards to call. Once you get on one bulletin board, it may have a list of other boards. These lists are not always kept up-to-date, however.

When you first get on a new board, its commands will flash by on the screen. Make a point of recording how to get out and how to get help. Either have your printer going or jot down the commands.

Since bulletin boards "wink" in and out of existence even faster than other segments of the computer world, check a new board's number with a voice phone call first. If the BBS has quit operation and the number has been reassigned, the human who answers is better off dealing with you than with your modem's high-pitched whistle.

Costs

Costs for the use of online services may include any or all of the following:

one-time membership charge

monthly service charge

hourly connect charge

minimum hourly connect charge per month

surcharge for special data bases or services

cost of user manual

telephone company charge

The public bulletin boards are an exception. A few boards, especially those that offer a lot of software, charge a one-time membership fee (typically $25) before giving the user a password. Some boards require a donation for certain services (usually software, sometimes leaving messages) but let you rummage around for free in other parts of the system.

B

The RS-232-C Interface

Pins important for the asynchronous serial communication typical of personal computers are **boldfaced**.

Table B-1.   RS-232-C Interface

Pin	Function	Direction		
1	**frame ground**	N/A		
2	**transmitted data**	DTE	>	DCE
3	**received data**	DTE	<	DCE
4	**request to send**	DTE	>	DCE
5	**clear to send**	DTE	<	DCE
6	**data set ready**	DTE	<	DCE
7	signal common	N/A		
8	data carrier detect	DTE	<	DCE
9	positive dc test voltage	N/A		
10	negative dc test voltage	N/A		
11	not assigned	N/A		
12	**speed indicator**	DTE	<	DCE
13	secondary clear to send	DTE	<	DCE
14	secondary transmitted data	DTE	>	DCE
15	serial clock transmit	DTE	<	DCE
16	secondary received data	DTE	<	DCE
17	serial clock receive	DTE	<	DCE
18	receiver dibit clock	DTE	<	DCE
19	secondary request to send	DTE	>	DCE
20	**data terminal ready**	DTE	>	DCE
21	signal quality detect	DTE	<	DCE
22	**ring indicator**	DTE	<	DEC
23	data rate select	varies		
24	external transm. clock	DTE	>	DCE
25	busy out	DTE	<	DCE

C

Further Reading: A Select List of Books

General

Knight, Timothy Orr. *The World Connection*. Indianapolis, Ind. Howard W. Sams, 1983.

Silveria, Terry C. and Sanjiva K. Nash. *The Buyer's Guide to Modem and Communications Software*. Blue Ridge Summit, Pa. Tab Books, 1985.

Kelly-Bootle, Stan. *The Devil's DP Dictionary*. New York. McGraw-Hill Book Company, 1981.

Computer-specific Communications Books

Ryan, Lee F. and Andrew Townsend. *The Kaypro Connection*. Blue Ridge Summit, Pa. Tab Books, 1985.

Erickson, Jonathan. *C-64 Telecommunications*. Berkeley, Ca. Osborne/McGraw-Hill, 1985.

Kruglinski, David. *The Osborne/McGraw Hill Guide to IBM PC Communications*. Berkeley, Ca. Osborne/McGraw-Hill, 1984.

Schwaderer, W. David. *Digital Communications Programming on the IBM PC*. New York. John Wiley and Sons, 1984.

> Excellent introductory chapters on modems. Most of book consists of BASIC communications programs.

Online Services

Davies, Owen and Mike Edelhart. *Omni Online Database Directory 1985.* New York. Macmillan, 1984.

> Comprehensive; updated annually.

Cane, Mike. *The Computer Phone Book.* New York. New American Library, 1983.

Stone, M. David. *Getting On-Line: A Guide to Accessing Computer Information Services.* Englewood Cliffs, N.J. Prentice-Hall, 1984.

Chandler, David. *Dialing for Data: A Consumer's How-To Handbook on Computer Communications.* New York. Random House, 1984.

> Good writing and good information. You may or may not
> like the author's taste in engravings.

Hansen, Carol. *The Microcomputer User's Guide to Information Online.* Hasbrouck Heights, N.J. Hayden, 1984.

Howitt, Doran and Marvin I. Weinberger. *Inc. Magazine's Databasics: Your Guide to Online Business Information.* New York. Garland Publishing, 1984.

Bowen, Charles and David Peyton. *How to Get the Most out of CompuServe.* New York. Bantam, 1984.

D

Glossary

ACOUSTIC COUPLER, ACOUSTIC COUPLED MODEM. A stand-alone modem with two cups in which a standard handset (telephone receiver and transmitter) fits. The modem generates sound waves that go in the telset.

ASCII. American Standard Code for Information Interchange. A commonly used computer operations code that assigns a numeric value to all upper- and lowercase letters of the alphabet, numerals, and certain nonprinting characters, such as bell, carriage return, and line feed. ASCII code is usually implemented as seven bits, yielding 128 characters. Eight-bit ASCII code, with 256 characters, can include graphics and other special characters. The assignments of characters above number 128 vary. ASCII tables are included in most computer manuals and general books about personal or home computers.

ASCII FILE. A text file consisting of seven-bit ASCII characters, usually created with a simple text editor. An ASCII file is distinguished from a word-processing file, which is created using word-processing software and is also text but may use eight-bit characters.

ASYNCHRONOUS. Not synchronized. In reference to data communications, asynch is the typical means of communication between small computers. Each character, coded as a string of bits, is sent separately with an indeterminate amount of time between characters. The beginning and end of a character are indicated by special start and stop bits. See also Data transmission bit, Serial, Synchronous, Start, and Stop bits.

AUTODIAL. A modem feature enabling the user to dial a telephone number from the computer's keyboard or from a program stored in the computer's or the modem's memory. Users whose modems lack this feature must dial the number on a regular telephone telset.

BANDWIDTH. A range or band of frequencies.

BAUD RATE. A term referring to the speed of communications between computers. Properly, baud rate refers to the number of signal changes on a communications line but frequently this term is understood to be identical with bits per second. Named after Jean-Maurice-Emile Baudot (1845-1903), who patented a five-digit telegraph code in 1874 that supplanted Morse code internationally in the twentieth century. Baudot also invented multiplexing for high-speed telegraphy (simultaneous transmission of several messages on the same channel).

BINARY FILE. Typically programs or executable files (those with extensions such as .COM, .EXE, .BAS, or .C).

BLOCK. A set number of bytes sent as a unit by an error-checking protocol.

BPS. Bits per second, which is a way of measuring the speed of computer-to-computer communication.

BUG. An undocumented feature. (Stan Kelly-Bootle, *The Devil's DP Dictionary*. New York: McGraw-Hill, 1981.)

BULLETIN BOARD (ELECTRONIC BULLETIN BOARD). A system consisting of a computer and modem with appropriate software, which users may call on the public telephone network. Analogous to public bulletin boards in laundromats and company lunchrooms, these electronic bulletin boards allow users to post notices and receive answers. A bulletin board may also have different levels of access, perhaps based on fees, password protection, and software available at little or no cost. Often abbreviated as BBS.

CALLBACK. A security feature of modems and communications software. When someone calls into a system that has this feature, he or she must leave a phone number for the system to call back. The system checks the number against a list of approved numbers before calling the person back.

CCITT. Consultative Committee for International Telegraphy and Telephony, a body operating under the United Nations' International Telecommunications Union, advising on standards in this area.

CHECKSUM. Used in error-checking protocols. Different protocols base the checksum on different aspects of the data. The receiving system compares its own checksum with the one from the sending system.

COM PORT. A COMmunications port—an interface on the computer that is used for exchanging information with another piece of equipment, such as a modem or a printer.

COMMAND MODE. In this mode, characters that the user enters on the keyboard are interpreted as commands by the user's own system. Contrasted with data or terminal mode in which the characters that the user enters are sent to the remote system.

CRC. Cyclic redundancy checking, which is a method of error checking.

DATA BIT. One of the seven or eight (for some systems, five or six) bits making up the code for a letter, number, or nonprinting character.

Data link. Two modems, each receiving and/or sending data from an attached computer, using a telephone line to send and/or receive data from each other.

Data mode. Contrasted with command mode: In data mode, characters the user enters on the keyboard are sent out to the online remote system. In command mode, characters the user enters are interpreted as commands by the user's own system.

Contrast with voice mode: Some modems and communications software allow users to switch back and forth between human-to-human communication, using a telephone plugged into the proper connector on the modem, and computer-to-computer communication, all without redialing. The computer-to-computer form is data mode.

DB-25 connector. A connector with 25 pins arranged in two rows. This connector can be used for an RS-232-C serial interface.

DCE. Data Communications Equipment, usually a modem. According to the RS-232 standard, DCE *receives* RTS (ready to send) and should send data on pin 3 and receive on pin 2.

Dibit. A pair of bits sent at one time.

Dibit encoded phase shift keying. The method by which 1200-bps modems send data. A pair of bits is indicated by a relative phase shift of the signal.

DIP switches. DIP is an acronym for Dual Inline Package. DIP switches are small switches in a printed circuit board that allow the user to set certain hardware options. Two types exist: slide and rocker.

Download. A term from the mainframe world for transmitting a file from a host computer to a (satellite) terminal. As applied to microcomputers, the system being called, such as an online service, an electronic bulletin board, or a computer at a place of business, is the "mainframe" sending a file, and the caller's personal computer acts like a terminal receiving the "downloaded" file.

DTE. Data Terminal Equipment, usually a terminal or computer. According to the RS-232 standard, DTE *sends* RTS (ready to send) and should send data on pin 2 and receive on pin 3.

Duplex. Two-way communication on one line. If transmission can be both ways at the same time, like a regular two-way street, communication is full duplex. Transmission one way at a time, like certain designated lanes or streets at rush hour, is half duplex. Transmission that is always in the same direction, like a regular one-way street, is simplex. *See* also Half duplex mode.

Echo. Online systems, such as online services, data bases, and bulletin boards, will send a caller's characters back to the caller's screen.

Therefore, the caller's system does not need to send, or echo, outgoing characters to its own screen.

If a microcomputer user is communicating with a system that does not send the characters back, such as a terminal that does not have the capability to do so, the user's system must echo the characters in order for the user to see them, which is *local echo* or *local copy*. If the remote system is sending the characters back and the user also has local echo on, the characters will be doubled, lliikkee tthhiiss.

ERROR-CHECKING PROTOCOL. A data communications protocol for exchanging files that, as it goes, checks for errors in a preset segment (block) of the file being sent, then retransmits any segment where transmission errors were found. Examples of error-checking data communications protocols are parity, XMODEM, Kermit, MNP, X.25, and X.PC.

EXTERNAL MODEM. *See* Stand-alone modem.

FLOW CONTROL CHARACTERS. Flow control characters enable a receiving system to stop the flow of information from another system. Usually used so that receiving system can catch up. Both systems must agree on the characters used. The most commonly used are CTRL S (ASCII value 19, hex 13) for stop and CTRL Q (ASCII value 17, hex 11) for restart. Flow control characters are also known as *XON/XOFF* characters.

FREEWARE. A term trademarked by the Headlands Communications Corporation to designate a way of marketing copyrighted software. Users send payment for the product after trying it and finding it useful. They may copy the program for others but not sell it. This concept represents a software marketplace version of the honor system.

FULL DUPLEX. *See* Duplex.

GATEWAY SERVICE. A computer system that a user can dial on the public telephone network and use to gain entry into specific online systems, such as electronic data bases. Gateway systems are usually easier to learn and use than the data bases to which these systems provide access.

HALF DUPLEX. *See* Duplex.

HALF DUPLEX MODE. Properly, local echo or local copy. In this mode, the computer echoes its own characters to the screen as well as sending them on the telephone line. Local echo is associated with half duplex communication because the systems that communicate only in that way also can't echo characters back to a sending system.

HANDSET. The part of the telephone telset containing the receiver and transmitter.

HANDSHAKE. For communication with modems, the exchange of signals occurring after the modem being called is online (answered). This exchange ensures that the data link is complete and data can be sent and received.

INTERFACE. The point at which two systems interact.

INTEGRAL MODEM. A modem built into a computer, especially a lapsize computer, and included in the price of the computer system.

INTERNAL MODEM. Modem in the form of a printed circuit board not enclosed in a case that is purchased separately from a computer and that can be inserted into an expansion slot in a personal computer. Usually packaged with a telephone cable and an external power supply.

KERMIT. A copyrighted, non-public-domain communications protocol with error checking. Developed at Columbia University for asynchronous ASCII or binary file transfer. Kermit bases its checksum either on the two's complement (like XMODEM), the one's complement, or cyclic redundancy checking. Kermit retransmits a block in case of error. This protocol can transmit data words of several formats.

LOCAL COPY, LOCAL ECHO. *See* Echo.

MARK. A term evolving from telegraphy, signifying a one bit or low signal.

MNP. Created and sold by Microcom, Inc., an error-checking protocol that is especially useful at the transmission speed of 2400 bps. This protocol uses 16-bit cyclic redundancy checking.

MODEM. An electronic device enabling computers to exchange information using the standard public telephone network. The sending modem *modulates* the computer's digital information into analog form for the telephone line. The receiving modem at the other end *demodulates* this analog information into digital information for use by the computer at the other end.

NULL. The first character in the ASCII code (000). Not the same as zero. Zero carries meaning, but null does not. The function of null usually is to allow the print head on an older model printer enough time to return to the left margin of the paper so that it can print the next line being sent. Some communications programs allow the user to set the number of nulls needed.

OFF HOOK, ON HOOK. Taking the handset (the part of the telephone telset that contains the receiver and transmitter) off the cradle is taking the telephone *off hook*. This connects the user to the telephone network so that a call can be placed. To terminate a call, the handset is placed *on hook* again. These terms apply just as well to modems. The OH light on some stand-alone modems stands for off hook.

ONLINE. The state in which a computer is connected via modem to another computer.

ONLINE DATA BASE, ONLINE SERVICE, ONLINE SYSTEM. A computer system that a user can dial through the public telephone network, with or without first paying a fee. Online services include CompuServe and The Source. Online data bases include Dialog and BRS. Online systems include all four and also electronic bulletin boards. *See* Appendix A.

ORIGINATE. Modem hardware term for "to place a call" as distinguished from answer.

PARITY. A simple method of error checking, using a bit following the data bits and preceding the stop bit. Parity may be even, odd, none, or, less frequently, mark or space. For even parity, whether the parity bit is a one or a zero depends on the data bits: If they add up to an even number such as 1110001 = 4, the parity bit for even parity will be zero. If they add up to an odd number, such as 1001100 = 3, the parity bit is one to make an even total (here, 4).

PASSWORD. A device aimed at encouraging free and open cooperation among the staff. (Stan Kelly-Bootle, *The Devil's DP Dictionary*. New York: McGraw-Hill, 1981.)

PORT ADDRESS. A number in the section of the computer reserved for input/output. Communications software uses this number to address instructions and data to the port.

PROTOCOL. An agreed-on set of rules. For personal computer communications, two kinds of protocols are important. The *dialing protocol* governs how the computer sends commands to the modem. Examples of dialing protocols are Hayes and Racal-Vadic. The *data transfer protocol* governs how data is sent and received. Examples are XMODEM, Kermit, MNP and X.25.

PULSE DIALING. The older method of dialing a telephone, which was used on rotary telsets (telephones). Pulses represent each digit of a telephone number, with the exception of the number 0, which is ten pulses. *See* Tone dialing.

REMOTE SYSTEM. The computer system at the other end of a communications link or line.

RINGBACK. The signal received by a caller (whether human or modem), which is generated by the branch of the telephone company at the receiver's end, that sounds like the ringing of the other telset.

RS-232-C. Recommended Standard number 232, revision C, of the Electronic Industry Association, determining the function of the 25 pins for a serial interface.

SERIAL DATA TRANSMISSION. Method of transmission wherein the bits carrying the information are sent one at a time, "Indian file," on a channel such as a telephone line.

SHAREWARE. Much like Freeware, which see.

Space. A term evolving from telegraphy, signifying a zero bit or high signal.

Stand-alone modem. A modem board housed in a metal or plastic case. To be attached to a computer with a serial cable. Stand-alone modems are usually packaged with a power supply that plugs into a power source and a telephone cable to connect the modem to the telephone network.

Start bit. In asynchronous communication, the bit that signals to the receiving system which data bits follow.

Stop bit. In asynchronous communication, the bit or bits (no more than two) that signal(s) to the receiving system the end of the incoming data bits.

Synchronous. A method of data communication with the internal clocks of the sending and receiving computers synchronized.

Telset. A more exact term for what is commonly called a telephone. The part of the telephone that the user picks up and that contains the receiver and transmitter is called the handset.

Terminal emulation. The state of adaptation necessary for a personal computer to act like a terminal, whether it be a TTY (dumb) terminal or a specific terminal with specialized keys.

Terminal mode. When a computer is online (connected) to another system, the computer is in terminal mode, and characters that the user enters on the computer's keyboard are sent to the remote system. Terminal mode is called data mode also. In *command mode*, by contrast, the characters the user enters are interpreted as commands by the user's own system.

Tone dialing. Dialing system in which a combination of two tones represents each digit in a telephone number. This system is used by pushbutton telephone handsets.

UART. Universal Asynchronous Receiver/Transmitter: an integrated circuit that converts parallel data from the computer into serial data for a serial device, such as a modem and also converts serial data into parallel data. In addition, this circuit also adds start, parity, and stop bits to outgoing data and strips them from incoming data, checking parity as needed.

USART. Universal Synchronous/Asynchronous Receiver/Transmitter: an integrated circuit that converts parallel data from the computer into serial data for a serial device, such as a modem, and also converts serial data into parallel data. Besides adding and removing start, parity, and stop bits for asynchronous communication, a USART adds and detects synchronous filler or other characters for synchronous communication.

UPLOAD. Mainframe term for transmitting a file to the host computer from a (satellite) terminal. As applied to microcomputers, the system being called, such as an online service, an electronic bulletin board, or a computer at a place of business, represents the mainframe receiving an uploaded file, and the caller's personal computer acts like a terminal sending the file. Contrasted with Download, which see.

WORM. A fiendish bit of hidden programming that can destroy all the data on the floppy or hard disk on which it is copied.

XMODEM. A version of a public domain communications protocol. Originally developed by Ward Christensen for asynchronous ASCII or binary file transfer on CP/M systems. XMODEM uses longitudinal redundancy checking with blocks of 128 characters, a checksum, and retransmission in case of error. Characters are formatted as one start bit, eight data bits, no parity bit, and one stop bit. The checksum is the sum of the SOH (start of header) character, the block number, the block number two's complement (one's complement in certain versions) and the 128 bytes of eight-bit data in the block.

XON/XOFF. The flow control characters CTRL S (ASCII value 19, hex 13) for stop and CTRL Q (ASCII value 17, hex 11) for restart. *See* Flow control characters.

X.PC. A subset of the X.25 error-checking protocol used in wide area networks. Created by the Tymnet public data network, X.PC allows communications multitasking. X.PC uses 16-bit cyclic redundancy checking.

E

Troubleshooting

In this appendix, we describe what to do when things go wrong as well as the techniques and equipment you need to make your own cables.

What To Do When Your System Does Not Work

You have purchased your modem and connected it but things don't seem to be working the way they should. Most of the time you can use a logical approach to overcome your problems. Following are some suggestions that can help avoid wasted energy.

Make a Thorough Visual Inspection

Have you overlooked anything that is vital to your system? Look for an RS-232 plug that is half off or a phone cable that is unconnected on one end or in the wrong jack on the modem. Any service technician can tell you tales of everyday folks who forgot to look for the obvious before calling in the "heavy artillery."

Check the Easy Things First

You have a pretty good chance to find your problem with less aggravation if you follow this simple rule. Some people immediately begin dissecting anything that will come apart, which greatly increases the chances of damaging sensitive electronic equipment. Professional technicians have seen cases where this "golden screwdriver syndrome" caused equipment with a minor problem to become "d.o.a."

Substitute

If you are unsure of the way something is supposed to function, you sometimes can get some insight by substituting a unit that you know works. Being able to borrow such equipment is made possible by friends groups, computer clubs, and so forth. If a known working unit doesn't work in your system, you have determined that the problem lies somewhere other than the unit. With this technique, you can use a process of elimination to find which part of your system is causing the problem.

Read the Manual

When in doubt, *read* the manual. This can be very enlightening.

Make Notes

Jot down any peculiarities about your problem. Such notes can help a professional pinpoint the problem more quickly, and time saved is money saved. Note any error messages that flashed on the screen, any smoke that might have come from your computer or modem, and any other event that is out of the ordinary.

Check COM Port Settings

Incorrect settings account for many problems. Due in part to a basic misunderstanding, as detailed in Chapter 2, the COM port is the address at which your computer can find your modem. Most PCs that have a built-in serial port, address it as COM 1. A notable exception is the PCjr, which calls the address of its serial port COM A If your modem COM port is not what the software is set for, commands from the software are routed to the wrong place and the modem does not respond because it never receives the commands.

For some problems you may see an indication that your computer is online when it is not, which usually means the program uses Pin 8 to detect the presence of carrier. The software interprets pin 8 going high as being online. A wrong COM address can make pin 8 "float," which means that when pin 8 is not connected to a DCE device, that pin floats between 3 and 15 Volts and looks like a valid carrier to the software so that the online message is sent. If you see this message and your modem does not seem to be obeying commands, doublecheck to make sure that your software is configured for the proper COM port address.

Many kinds of software can run data communications equipment at speeds ranging up to 9600 bps. If your modem does not seem to respond, make sure that you are sending to it at a speed that the modem can understand. To determine the correct speed, look in your software configurations or options menu.

Make sure that you do not have two peripherals set for the same COM port. This double setting can cause all kinds of weird symptoms, such as the modem dialing but never completing handshaking or failing to auto-answer. The "other" peripheral is usually a printer, and printers are usually COM 1.

Check Your Equipment

Problems can occur also at the 25-pin interface. To determine what is going on at this interface, you need a device known in the trade as a "breakout box." It is a small case, usually a folding type, that has a 25-pin connector at each end so that you can plug the box in series between the computer and the modem. LEDs (light-emitting diodes) are placed on the most important lines and will light when a signal is present. Breakout boxes usually have three banks of switches across the middle that allow the user to open the lines and cross them if desired. Crossing wires would be done when hardwiring two computers to allow them to communicate in back-to-back fashion, for example. This feature also allows you to find by experimentation the correct pinout for a nonstandard cable.

The cost of a breakout box is usually $100 and up. However, a similar and less expensive device exists. It does not have the switches but has the monitor LEDs. Called "quick-check", it costs about $69 as of this writing.

A breakout box can help you determine whether your commands are lighting the LED for pin 2, called TXD (Transmit Data). The modem then should respond as shown by a flash or the LED for pin 3 (Receive Data). If you do not see a response, make sure that you are using a software program which sends commands that your modem can understand. Many autodialing protocols exist, and the software and modem have to be able to communicate in like terms. Make sure also that your parity and stop bit settings are correct. Look in your user's manual if you are in doubt. However, using seven data bits, even parity, and one stop bit will almost always work.

If your software has a terminal mode, commands entered at the keyboard are sent out the serial port. You can command the modem directly by using the commands specified in your user's manual.

One of the important signals you can use your breakout box to look for is DTR (Data Terminal Ready), which is pin 20. This signal tells the modem that data terminal equipment is ready to begin communicating. Without this signal, the modem cannot autoanswer or originate. In some modems, a means exists to force this signal high, so if the DTE does not provide the signal, you may be able to use a modem. Barring that solution, you could still force the signal high by using a jumper wire from another pin that is continually held high, such as pin 9. Of course, once you find out what you need in the way of pinouts, you could make up a custom cable to fit your application.

If questions about your modem cannot be answered by reading the manual or asking your modem dealer, call the technical support number in the user's manual. Often this number is toll-free.

Making Your Own Cable

Soldering is not difficult (as you will see in the following). You are likely to find it less expensive to make a cable with solder type connectors than to buy one already made, and you will have the satisfaction of having made your cable yourself.

What Do You Need?

If you decide to give soldering a try, the following items will be helpful and necessary: soldering iron, solder, wire stripper, screwdriver, damp sponge, flux, electrical tape, and pliers. A small vise and soldering iron holder also will be helpful, although you can do without them. You can find these supplies at an electronics or hardware store. In fact, you may have most of the equipment already if you like to tinker with electronics. The main ingredients are, of course, solder and the soldering iron (with a large dose of patience—rushing doesn't pay). Remember that soldering is easy. Its only three requirements are 1) everything must be clean, 2) a proper solder must be used (more about this when we get to the discussion on solder itself), and 3) sufficient heat must be produced.

What Is Soldering?

Before we get started, a bit of background to soldering will be helpful. Soldering can be defined as the process of uniting two clean pieces of metal with a thin layer of a third metal applied in a molten state. Three types of soldering are used in metal work: brazing, silver soldering, and soft soldering. This last method is practiced in electrical and electronic work. The solder alloy used in electronics work is usually 60 percent tin and 40 percent lead and comes in wire form. The ratio of tin to lead content determines the hardness, strength, and melting point of the solder.

Getting Ready

Use the Jump Table to determine which cable connection diagram you should use for your particular modem/computer combination (see Chapter 5 for an explanation of how to use the charts). Once you have determined which diagram to use, you will see which type of connectors and cable you need to buy. After you obtain the connectors and cable, color code your drawing. For instance: red goes from pin 1 on the modem side to pin 1 on the computer side, brown from pin 2 on the modem side to pin 4 on the computer side, green from 4 to 7, white from 5 to 9, and so on. The color coding is arbitrary, just be consistent for each cable that you make. Once you have color coded your diagram and laid out the connectors, you are almost ready to make a cable.

In order to ready the cable ends for soldering, all insulation, along with grease, oil, scale, oxides, or other foreign matter must be removed for a good hold. Obviously, you remove the insulation with wire strippers or any grease with a sponge, but how about oxides? A flux is used to remove oxides thus ensuring a good solder joint. The flux used in electronics work is resin. Often the wire type of solder will have at least one core of flux, but you may want to get a separate tin of resin flux just to ensure clean connections. Note that acid or soldering paste should *never* be used as flux for soldering electronic joints. After a period of time, these harsh cleaning agents would corrode the delicate wires and connections.

Now on to the soldering iron itself. The soldering iron's tip is its most important feature. You will want a small, flat tip for connecting your modem-computer cable's wires. Many soldering irons have a removeable tip that may be unscrewed and replaced with another, more convenient size later.

Soldering

The wire ends are stripped and cleaned, the connectors marked and ready, and you have at hand the proper cabling diagram for you modem/ computer combination. Plug in your soldering iron, make sure the tip is not resting on anything flammable. If you have a soldering iron holder, use it. Let the iron heat sufficiently so that it will easily melt the solder. Unless the tip of your iron is pre-tinned, you will have to tin the tip. Tinning is accomplished by spreading a thin layer of molten solder over the metal tip. This solder penetrates the surface of the tip to a molecular depth, forming a thin cushion of molten solder through which heat can be transferred (see Fig. E-1).

Fig. E-1.   **Tinning the iron.**

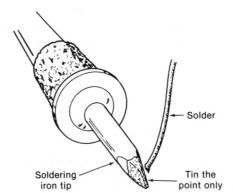

Solder

Soldering iron tip

Tin the point only

Whenever possible the wire ends of the cable to be soldered should be tinned first (do not try to tin the connector ends). Tinning enables the solder to penetrate to a molecular depth and allows a thorough bond between the solder, the wire end, and the connector.

The cable connectors we recommend for solder-type connections have solder pots (see Fig. E-2). These solder pots are actually the rear end of the contact pins for your modem/computer cable. The wire ends are inserted into the properly numbered pots and soldered. However, before the actual soldering can begin, the pots must be prepared by partially filling them with a small amount of molten solder. This solder should be introduced into the solder pot as shown in Figure E-3.

Fig. E-2. **Typical cable connectors.**

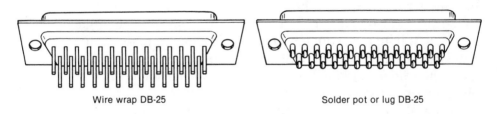

Wire wrap DB-25   Solder pot or lug DB-25

Fig. E-3. **Filling solder pots.**

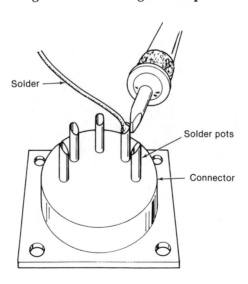

If you have a vise, clamp the cable connector in the vise, then partially fill the pots that correspond to your modem/computer cable diagram. If you do not have a vise, use pliers. The vise frees one hand and enables you to make your cables without a lot of gymnastics. If you plan to make more than one or two cables, seriously consider purchasing a vise.

Another way to place solder in the solder pot is to cut a piece of solder to a length shorter than the height of the pot and drop the piece into the pot. The solder pot is heated, and the solder inside melts. Please note that the amount of solder in the pot should never completely fill the pot (at least until the wire end is in place). Remember that a little solder is much better than a lot!

Now a wire from the cable that was previously cut to size and tinned may be inserted in the solder pot by reheating and melting the solder in the pot. A properly soldered connector is illustrated in Figure E-4. You should repeat this procedure for each connection required for your particular modem/computer combination. Be sure that you do not hold the soldering iron tip to the soldering pot for too long, or you might melt the plastic that holds the contact pin and solder pot in place. Solder remelts quickly, so a delicate touch with the iron to the pot is all that is required to make the solder in the pot liquid again. Between soldering connections, wipe the tip of the soldering iron on the damp sponge. The tip will build up material, mostly burnt resin, that will interfere with your soldering.

Fig. E-4.   Properly soldered connector.

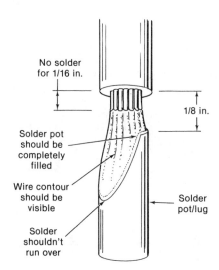

No solder for 1/16 in.

1/8 in.

Solder pot should be completely filled

Wire contour should be visible

Solder pot/lug

Solder shouldn't run over

When you complete all the connections, you are ready to attach the cable connector covers and use your cable. Cable connector covers come in two main styles: the screw-down type and the clip type. The screw-down-type covers require a screwdriver, are a bit more flexible (and usually cost more), and the clip covers simply snap in place. Once your covers are in place, connect your cable, adjust the DIP switch settings (as described in Chapter 5) and start communicating.

Summary: What You Really Need to Know About Cable Making

You see that cable making is not difficult. Soldering makes the best connections and requires only a bit of patience; all surfaces thoroughly cleaned and tinned; a good soldering iron with a small, flat tip used with prudence; and a solder with the proper tin-to-lead content and the proper flux.

By using the soldering hints in this appendix and the general knowledge about how modems and computers function together in this book, you are ready to make any of the cables described in the diagrams in Chapter 5 and even go on to figure out your own!

F

Communications Software for Microcomputers

Apple II + , IIe, IIc

Kermit: Columbia University Center for Computing Activities, New York

Applesoft: Apple Computer, Inc., Cupertino, Ca

Access II: Apple Computer, Inc., Cupertino, Ca

Appleterm: Apple Computer, Inc., Cupertino, Ca

Smartcom: Hayes Microcomputer Products, Inc., Norcross, Ga

pfs:Access: Software Publishing Company, Mountain View, Ca

ASCII Express: United Software Industries, Century City, Ca

Macintosh

Kermit: Columbia University Center for Computing Activities, New York

Smartcom: Hayes Microcomputer Products, Inc., Norcross, Ga

MacTerminal: Apple Computer, Inc., Cupertino, Ca

Dow Jones Straight Talk: Dow Jones Software, Princeton, NJ

MacGeorge: Racal Data Communications Inc. (Racal-Vadic),
Milpitas, Ca

CP/M

(Apple II family, Kaypro, Osborne, Morrow Micro Decision)

XMODEM, Modem7: public domain

Kermit: Columbia University Center for Computing Activities,
New York

Crosstalk 3.0: Microstuf, Inc., Atlanta, Ga

MITE: Mycroft Labs Inc., Tallahassee, Fl

IBM PC Family and Compatibles

(IBM PC, XT, AT, PC portable, PCjr)

Kermit: Columbia University Center for Computing Activities,
New York

PC-TALK III: The Headlands Communications, Tiburon, Ca

Crosstalk XVI: Microstuf Inc., Atlanta, Ga

Smartcom: Hayes Microcomputer Products, Inc., Norcross, Ga

pfs:Access: Software Publishing Co., Mountain View, Ca

GEORGE 2.0: Racal Data Communications Inc. (Racal-Vadic),
Milpitas, Ca

MITE: Mycroft Labs Inc., Tallahassee, Fl

Relay: VM Personal Computing Corp., New York

Index

MORE
FROM
SAMS

☐ Mastering Serial Communications

This intermediate/advanced book is written for technicians and programmers interested in asynchronous serial communications. Part One explains the history and technical details of asynchronous communications, while Part Two addresses the specifics of the technical programmer with an emphasis on popular UARTS and pseudo-assembly language. Contents: Introduction, ASCII, The Serial World View, The UART, The Serial Interface, Modems, Applications Software, Serial Communications Programming. Joe Campbell.
ISBN 0-672-22450-X $21.95

☐ Personal Computer Troubleshooting and Repair Guides

If you have some knowledge of electronics, these easy-to-understand repair and maintenance guides provide the instructions you need to repair your Apple® II + /IIe, IBM® PC, or Commodore 64™ computer. Contains schematic diagrams, block diagrams, photographs and troubleshooting flowcharts to trace the probable cause of failure. A final chapter on advanced troubleshooting shows you how to perform more complicated repairs.
APPLE II + /IIe
ISBN 0-672-22353-8 . . . . $19.95
IBM PC
ISBN 0-672-22358-9 . . . . $19.95
COMMODORE 64
ISBN 0-672-22363-5 . . . . $19.95

☐ 68000, 68010, 68020 Primer

The newest 68000 family of chips, found in Apple's Lisa® and Macintosh™ and IBM's 3270 PC, is covered in this timely and up-to-date primer. This user-friendly guide gives you a complete understanding of Motorola's powerful microprocessor chip and features actual programming examples, such as file locking and data handling techniques. For the beginner as well as the more experienced programmer.
Kelly-Bootle and Fowler.
ISBN 0-672-22405-4 . . . . $21.95

☐ Printer Connections Bible

At last! A book that teaches non-technical people how to connect a computer to a printer. Covers major computer/printer combinations, supplies detailed diagrams of required cables, DIP-switching settings, etc. The book is graphically oriented, with diagrams illustrating numerous printer/computer combinations. House and Marble.
ISBN 0-672-22406-2 . . . . $16.95

☐ Crash Course in Artificial Intelligence

A detailed self-study course in Artificial Intelligence. Discusses AI principles and methods, and provides introductory applications of AI through sample programs in Prolog and Lisp. An excellent book for programmers, students, and engineers who need a thorough understanding of AI. Louis Frenzel.
ISBN 0-672-22443-7 . . . . $21.95

☐ C Primer Plus

Who better to explain the intricacies of C and UNIX than the master of systems? It's Waite at his best. Provides a clear and complete introduction to the C programming language and guides you in the proper use of C programming methodology. Interfacing C with assembly language is included, as well as many sample programs usable with any standard C compiler. Build a sound working knowledge of the language with C Primer Plus. Waite, Prata, and Martin.
ISBN 0-672-22090-3 . . . . $22.95

☐ CP/M® Bible: The Authoritative Reference Guide to CP/M

Already a classic, this highly detailed reference manual puts CP/M's commands and syntax at your fingertips. Instant one-stop access to all CP/M keywords, commands, utilities, and conventions are found in this easy-to-use format. If you use CP/M, you need this book. Waite and Angermeyer.
ISBN 0-672-22015-6 . . . . $19.95

☐ CP/M Primer (2nd Edition)

This tutorial companion to the CP/M Bible is highly acclaimed and widely used by novices and advanced programmers alike. Includes the details of CP/M terminology, operation, capabilities, internal structure, plus a convenient tear-out reference card with CP/M commands. This revised edition allows you to begin using new or old CP/M versions immediately in any application. Waite and Murtha.
ISBN 0-672-22170-5 . . . . $16.95

☐ Soul of CP/M: How to Use the Hidden Power of Your CP/M System

Recommended for those who have read the CP/M Primer or who are otherwise familiar with CP/M's outer layer utilities. This companion volume teaches you how to use and modify CP/M's internal features, including how to modify BIOS and use CP/M system calls in your own programs. Waite and Lafore.
ISBN 0-672-22030-X $19.95

MORE
FROM
SAMS

MORE
FROM
SAMS